Stephen N. Merrill

The New Testament Idea of Hell

Vol. 1

Stephen N. Merrill

The New Testament Idea of Hell
Vol. 1

ISBN/EAN: 9783337389963

Printed in Europe, USA, Canada, Australia, Japan

Cover: Foto ©Lupo / pixelio.de

More available books at **www.hansebooks.com**

THE

NEW TESTAMENT IDEA

OF

HELL.

BY

Sr Mr MERRILL, D. D.,

Bishop of the Methodist Episcopal Church.

PREFACE.

THIS little book is written for readers of the English Scriptures, and not for those having access to the wide range of theological discussions found in the ponderous works on Systematic Divinity, which crowd the libraries of the learned. It therefore avoids, as far as possible, the use of foreign words and elaborate criticisms, keeping an eye to the needs of ordinary inquirers and seeking to lead them to the knowledge of the meaning and use of the original terms translated Hell in the New Testament.

No pretension is made to having discovered any meaning in those words, or any fact in regard to their origin, history, or use not previously known, and not well established in the minds of all who have given particular attention to the subject. The reader will find, however, that the Scriptures containing them are classified a little differently, and that the terms are so applied as to bring their specific differences into greater prominence and into right relations. This is one of the chief features of the work, and if this aim is realized the result will be accepted as a sufficient reason for its publication. It will enable the reader of moderate culture to study the subject intelligently, knowing in every instance whether the passage in hand relates to *Hades*, *Tartarus*, or *Gehenna*, an advantage not to be lightly esteemed.

Some will be disappointed in finding so little said directly upon those knotty questions which arise in connection with the subject of future punishment, and it may not be satisfactory to be told that such discussions have been purposely omitted, in order to keep attention to those points which relate to the *fact* itself, and which are necessarily preliminary to the consideration of the nature and duration of punishment, and of the methods adopted for the vindication of the divine proceeding which inflicts the penalty of eternal death upon the impenitent. But the course pursued accords with the writer's best judgment, and will be appreciated when the scope and design of the volume are taken into the account. One fault with many writers on this subject is, that they too readily plunge into the mysteries which baffle the keenest intellect and the stoutest heart.

The first thing necessary is to clear the subject of embarrassments, by ascertaining as nearly as possible what the Scriptures teach. In many instances this will remove the most serious difficulties from the mind, for the reason that those difficulties arise from misconceptions of the truth, or from wrong impressions in regard to it. The next thing of importance is to study carefully what is proposed for our acceptance in lieu of that which we find in the Scriptures. Just here many miss their footing. They listen to broad assertions, and reject unpalatable truth because it is unpalatable, without looking whither they are drifting or where they are to land. Human life is a fact, sin is a fact, the approach of death is a fact, and entrance into the unseen world is a fact. The Scriptures tell us what is there to be expected. Men object. They quibble; but they do not change the facts, nor bring us clearer light, or point us to firmer ground.

In this little book *Hades* is treated as a fact. The word itself is of little consequence. The fact exists. It is a world unseen, but real, and it would have existed and filled its office, if the name had been different, or if no name had ever been given to it. The Mississippi River poured its waters along the same channel for ages before the word Mississippi was known, and it would have continued as deep and wide if no name had been applied to it. So with the invisible world. It does not depend on its name for existence or character. In the course of human events, and perchance of human follies, it so happened that the word *Hades* was used among men as the name of the unknown regions inhabited by departed souls; and the Savior adopted it as suitable to his purpose, because it would be understood, and in using it he sanctioned the general idea of a world of spirits, without sanctioning the fanciful notions prevailing in regard to its location, or the pursuits of its inhabitants, because these ideas were neither contained in the name nor conveyed by its use. The origin of the word, and its use prior to its application to the nether world, is of no significance, except as showing how it took the meaning it bore in the days of Christ, and how it became suitable for his purpose.

The same remark is true of *Gehenna*. The name is a mere incident. The eternal state of the wicked is a fact — a necessity. Its terribleness grows out of the nature of sin, and the relation of sin to the divine government. The word *Gehenna* has nothing to do with the nature of sin, and sheds no light on the problem of evil. It only happened, by a very natural process, to become so related to the punishment of sin, in the mind of the Jewish people, that it could be very easily carried over into the eternal state, and applied metaphorically to the final perdition of the ungodly. This was done before Christ came, and he adopted the word and used it in that sense. The use of the word elsewhere, and before it received this application, is of no consequence. The punishment it denotes does not depend on the name; nor does the name reveal the cause or degree of the punishment. We study the name in view of its uses, and we gather all our ideas of the punishment from the surroundings of the word, and its application, knowing that all that to which it applies might have existed and been revealed under some other name, as we claim it does exist, and has been made known without reference to this name. The name presupposes the thing, but does not determine its nature or qualities. The use of the word is every thing. It is applied to a state of punishment, and the incidents of the punishment are so distinctly marked as to render it certain that the punishment is after death, and yet not in the separate state, but in the final state, where soul and body share the retribution.

In most discussions of future punishment, the terms which express duration occupy large space; but in these pages, those terms are not mentioned. They are not forgotten, however, nor is any theory advanced that ignores or disregards them. They are simply not reached. They were not necessary to the end in view, if pertinent to the present purpose, and it was deemed best not to overload the argument under this title, especially as another volume is in contemplation, as soon as pressing duties will permit its preparation.

The theories claiming consideration in this connection are numerous. That which represents all punishment as reformatory, and necessarily limited as to duration, leads all the others, and commands the largest share of attention. It assumes a post-mortem probation, and sets up a new standard of retribution, unknown to the Scriptures—namely, not according to *deeds*, but according to *needs*. Its fundamental thought is, that men are punished just enough to reform them, and with that sole object in view. This theory is deficient in philosophy and in Scripture warrant. We find no room for probation after death, but such facts established, and such principles alleged, as preclude the possibility of such a thing.

The soul-sleeping and annihilation theories have been encountered only incidentally, and refuted so far as the necessity of the argument required. They belong more properly to the discussion of the nature of punishment. The Scriptural idea, however, of the separate existence of the soul, has been presented, and thereby the crude philosophy of all materialistic conceptions of the soul has been antagonized.

The objections usually urged against eternal punishment are of two classes—those which arise out of false and unscriptural views of the subject, and those which are merely fault-finding and have no tendency to disprove the doctrine. Of the first class are those which perplexed Canon Farrar. His greatest trouble is with the "accretions," and especially the notion of "physical tortures," and the direct agency of God in tormenting the lost. In the outcome he does not deny that sin involves the condition of the soul in eternity, and may keep it out of heaven forever. The other objections are fallacious. They fault the thing itself, and stand with equal force whether the doctrine be true or false. They are aimed against the fact, and not against the proofs of the fact.

Of this class are those which depend on *a priori* reasonings. All arguments of this kind are necessarily inconclusive, for the reason that we are insufficiently acquainted with the premises to warrant us in affirming the conclusion. We can not comprehend the nature of God, and to reason from his nature is to reason from what we do not know. But some of God's attributes are revealed. He is just and holy, and we may safely reject any doctrine that arrays itself against justice and holiness. He is good and true, and we may and must reject any doctrine opposed to goodness and truth. This is all plain enough; but it is quite different from arguing from the divine nature, so imperfectly understood, to any conclusion with reference to the rightful method of revealing the justice and holiness of God, or with reference to the *degree* of punishment that is compatible with his goodness. This last requires not only the knowledge of the fact that God is holy and just and good, but the comprehension of the degree and power of these perfections, and also the comprehension of the nature and desert of sin as a disturbing element in the moral universe.

"Such knowledge is too wonderful for me; it is too high, I can not attain unto it." Therefore all reasoning from the nature of God to the nature or degree of the punishment which he can or can not inflict is reasoning from premises which are imperfectly and inadequately understood.

Some will imagine, no doubt, that too much attention has been given to the details of opposing opinions and expositions. Possibly this is true. Nevertheless, careful observation among those troubled by these things has convinced me that many pass too easily over these details, which appear so absurd to themselves, not realizing what influence ingenious quibbling has on minds just grappling for the first time with these questions, and doing it without antecedent training in the arts of reasoning, and without the knowledge of the rules of interpretation. Hundreds of minds are swayed by little things which seem unworthy of formal refutation. It is therefore well not to regard any thing too small to notice, which we have reason to believe appears formidable to other minds, and controls their decisions in relation to important questions.

The chapters on topics which do not necessarily belong to the use of the terms rendered Hell are added because of their connection with the general subject, and as illustrative of the thought that the essential fact of Hell is revealed independently of the use of these words. The theme is the same, and the pertinency of these chapters will be recognized on perusal of them in connection with the whole argument.

With the hope that this effort to set the subject in a clear light before the reader, so far as it is treated, will not be useless labor, this little volume is sent forth with the prayer that the blessing of God may attend it, and make it instrumental in leading many seekers after truth into safe and Scriptural views of the retributions of eternity.   S. M. M.

CHICAGO, ILL., July, 1878.

CONTENTS.

	PAGE.
I. THE TERMS EMPLOYED,	17
II. ERRORS ANTAGONIZED,	33
III. HADES—AUTHORITIES,	47
IV. HADES—SCRIPTURE USE,	64
V. THE SEPARATE EXISTENCE OF THE SOUL,	81
VI. SUFFERING IN HADES,	100
VII. FIXEDNESS OF CHARACTER IN HADES,	131
VIII. GEHENNA—THE ISSUE STATED,	147
IX. UNIVERSALIST EXPOSITIONS,	155
X. THE JEWISH BELIEF,	166
XI. GEHENNA—SCRIPTURE USE,	181
XII. GEHENNA—SCRIPTURE USE CONTINUED,	193
XIII. GEHENNA—SCRIPTURE USE CONTINUED,	205
XIV. THE LAKE OF FIRE,	228
XV. THE SECOND DEATH,	249
XVI. THE RESURRECTION OF DAMNATION,	257

New Testament Idea of Hell.

Chapter I.

THE TERMS EMPLOYED.

THE punishment of sinners is an alternative fact. It is God's "strange work," the last resort of his wisdom and goodness, the final expression of his holiness. It is never to be considered as the primary design of the law, or of the government which makes the law, or of the administrator bearing the responsibility of maintaining the public order for which the law and government exist. In it God takes no delight. Yet the necessities of good government, the maintenance of order under rightful authority, and the highest regard for the welfare of the good, require this ultimate vindication of righteousness at the expense of the incorrigibly wicked.

To the Bible alone do we look for light on this subject. There are voices in nature and voices in our own souls which speak with reference to it; but their utterances are indistinct and inharmonious, and without the authoritative teachings of the Scriptures these other revelations can not be safely interpreted. We therefore come to God's Word to learn the facts, so far as they are declared to us, and to accept the statements therein contained as final, so far as we can understand and apply them.

It is not to be expected, however, that our curiosity will be gratified. The more we learn of God and of his government, and of the dispensations of his providence, and of the moral relations of his creatures, and of the possibilities of destiny, the more deeply are we impressed with the incomprehensibleness of his nature, and the unfathomableness of his purposes. The light he gives us is the "true light." It is sufficient for our probational necessities. As a lamp to our feet, it will not misdirect our steps; but it does not scatter all the darkness from our surroundings, nor make luminous the entire pathway of our future being. We know in part. We see through a glass darkly. But the assurance is given that hereafter the fuller light will come, and with it will come the higher revelations of the divine glory, and the more perfect vindications of the divine government.

The subject of future punishment, in the nature of the case, is the hardest to understand. It grows out of moral conditions which are abnormal, and moral relations which are distorted. It belongs to the darker side of the divine dispensations. In every aspect in which we can view it, there is necessarily something beyond the apparent—something deeper and darker—something that evades our sight and thought, that recedes at our approach, and bids defiance to our wishes. We stand before it with awe. We look with amazement. A strange misgiving, an indefinable consciousness of timidity comes over us as we think of the insoluble mystery, and yet apprehend the dreadful reality of a world of woe. A thousand questions arise, and a thousand conjectures come and go, and yet the darkness is not driven away, nor the stubborn fact removed. It stands out before us in outline, commanding our attention, and yet refusing to disclose its interior form or furnishment. We study it as a mystery.

There are several features of this subject which have hitherto received much attention, and are worthy of it, but which, for lack of space in this little treatise, we will not at all consider. The nature, duration, and results of punishment in the future world will possibly afford a theme for another volume, but this one must be devoted to matters preliminary to the discussions which such a work would contain; namely, the fact of Hell. And by this term is meant a state of punishment beyond death, which is final, and from which there is no deliverance. I shall indulge no speculations concerning its location, its structure, or dimensions; but shall aim to follow the light of the Scriptures concerning the *fact*, and seek so to identify the fact as to be able rightly to apply all the passages bearing on the subject, each in order. This will avoid confusion of thought and of argument, a most important point. In a majority of instances this is not done. Many turn aside, unconsciously it may be, from the main question of *fact*, to its modes, its nature, its conditions, and then the difficulties that necessarily belong to these incidents are allowed to encumber the primary question, which ought to be settled, first of all, upon a sure foundation, supported by the testimonies which relate to it, independently of human conjectures, wishes, or prepossessions of any sort.

That there is confusion in the popular mind on the subject of Hell is not to be questioned. It exists in the Church and out of the Church, among the othodox and the heterodox, believers and unbelievers. It is found among the learned and the unlearned, and not one of us dares assume entire freedom from its influence. In our earlier thoughts we were undoubtedly biased by traditional impressions, which partook of the current opinions, and were shaped by them, without escaping the effect of those accretions which the truth had gathered to itself in its contact with human thoughts and passions. But all the crudities of opinion that have found currency are not chargeable to these early biases. Some are inevitable from the conditions of the subject, as found in our standard version of the Scriptures. Let us look at this a little. There are four words translated Hell in the Bible, and not one of them answers to the popular idea which has become nearly universal where the English Scriptures are read. This is a fact known to scholars conversant with the original, but scarcely suspected by the ordinary reader; and why should it be? He has no means of knowing, when he sees the word Hell, whether he has before him one or the other of these original words, and therefore he can not tell whether he is reading of *Hades* or *Gehenna*. The result is inevitable. He confounds things that differ. He applies passages indifferently that contain these different terms, and that ought not to be so applied.

Nor have those who read the original been as careful to classify the Scriptures containing these terms as the importance of the matter demands. Perhaps the majority of ministers apply those passages indiscriminately to the same state of being in which the different original terms are found. This is a mistake which is scarcely excusable. But it would not be so bad if the original terms were synonyms, or had a meaning so nearly alike that they could be used interchangeably in the language to which they belong. Such use of them would not then be misleading. But they can not be used interchangeably. They are not alike in origin, history, use, application, or meaning. And yet they are translated by the same English word. To say the least of it this is unfortunate and necessarily misleading.

The Old Testament word *Sheôl* is used with some latitude of meaning and application. It, however, always relates to the state of the dead, unless used in a metaphorical sense of something in this world; but sometimes it expresses the state of the body, and at other times of the soul. It does not express duration. It means in general the unseen world, the state of departed souls. It is not the decisive term in this discussion, and its use will occupy but little of our attention.

Tartarus occurs but once in the Scriptures, and will require but brief consideration. It is found in 2 Peter ii, 4: "For if God spared not the angels that sinned, but cast them down to hell—*Tartarus*—and delivered them into chains of darkness, to be reserved unto judgment," etc. It is the prison of the fallen angels, this side of the judgment, and should have been treated as a proper name—that is, it should have been transferred without translation. Then its meaning, as found in classic usage, and in the connection in which it is found, would have followed it and become familiar to all Biblical students.

Hades is a more important word. It occurs eleven times in the New Testament, and is translated "hell" ten times, and "grave" once. It is the Greek equivalent for the Hebrew *Sheôl*. When a passage is quoted in the New Testament from the Old, containing *Sheôl*, it is rendered by *Hades*. There is no disagreement among scholars as to the meaning of *Hades*. Some difference of application may be found, but, upon the whole, there is substantial agreement. This fact renders our task comparatively easy, so far as this word is concerned. It means the unseen world, the place of departed souls, and expresses nothing as to their character or condition. It always relates to the soul in a disembodied state, and never to the body; so that it should never be rendered grave. There are other Greek words that express the receptacle of the dead body, such as are rendered grave, tomb, sepulcher, etc.; but this word has no such meaning, and admits of nothing material. Hence, its true and only application is to the state of the dead, between death and the resurrection. This point is to be emphasized in this treatise.

Gehenna is the next word. It occurs in the New Testament twelve times, and, with a single exception, James iii, 6, where it is used metaphorically, it occurs in the discourses of our Lord alone. It related to the Jews, primarily, and would only be understood by them. Here, also, there is substantial agreement among scholars. The origin and meaning of the word are not in dispute. It is composed of two Hebrew words which together mean the valley of Hinnom. This was a place in the valley south of Jerusalem, once the seat of idolatrous worship, where stood the image of Moloch, where the Canaanites, and afterward the Israelites in their backslidden state, performed the cruel rites that distinguished the worship of that monstrous idol. King Josiah destroyed this worship, and polluted the place, so that it became the receptacle of the filth of the city. In the old Testament it was also called *Tophet*, in allusion to the beating of drums that was kept up during the worship of Moloch. The name of this place became the synonym of all that was opposed to God and hateful to his people, and very naturally came into use to express the Jewish idea of the punishment of the enemies of God after death. In this condition of things, and in this sense, our Savior used *Gehenna*, with reference to the ultimate punishment of the wicked. Its use comes nearer to the meaning which the popular sentiment attaches to the English word Hell than does any other of the terms so translated; and yet it is a proper name—the name of a place well-known—and should have been transferred, and not translated. The discussion of this word has reference, not to its origin, history, or meaning, but to its application. The questions raised are as to whether the Savior used it literally or figuratively; and whether he designed it to apply to punishment in this world, or the next world.

With those who believe in eternal punishment the practice is quite common of applying this word to the state immediately after death; that is, to punishment in *Hades;* but this is evidently improper. It should apply only to the *final state* of the wicked; and therefore, never to any state, or place, or condition this side of the resurrection of the dead. To correct this mistake, and to classify the Scriptures containing these different words so as to avoid the confusion that has resulted from their indiscriminate use, is largely the purpose of this volume. Indeed, this is about all that is necessary to the vindication of the Scriptural doctrine of retribution.

Here then is the arrangement to be observed. *Sheôl* is translated by *Hades;* and *Hades*, being the New Testament word, we take it in its truest sense, as applying to the invisible world, the state of the dead between death and the resurrection, and never to any thing beyond the resurrection. *Tartarus* is another word for the same thing, with only the difference that it is the prison of the fallen angels this side of the judgment. It is therefore substantially the same as *Hades*, and may be considered as a part of *Hades*. In other words, *Hades* covers the entire ground this side of the resurrection. *Gehenna* applies to nothing till *Hades* is past. It relates to the period beyond the resurrection and the judgment, the final state. This is the true distinction and it is certainly plain, and easily comprehended, and quite as easily demonstrated.

Not one of these words expresses duration. This is simply a fact, and to state it is no concession to any one, or to any doctrine. The idea of duration is incidental and consequential. *Hades* has duration, of necessity, as this world has, and as any thing has which has being. Its duration is limited, so far as humanity is concerned, to the period of this world's history, or to the time of the existence of souls in the disembodied state. In the resurrection it will give up its dead, and pass away, at least so far as we are concerned. Therefore the punishment in it is not forever. And, therefore, those who prove that *Hades* is not a place of eternal punishment, have not gained a point, as they suppose they have, against the orthodox teaching, because they have not met the issue in dispute.

So *Gehenna* has duration, though it is not expressed by the word. The duration is implied. But the state to which it applies is in eternity. It is beyond the resurrection. And there is no great fact beyond it. There is neither resurrection nor judgment to follow. So far as the Scriptures indicate, there is no limit to the state expressed by *Gehenna*. It follows from all this that *Hades* and *Gehenna* are quite different, and that they must be so recognized and treated, in order to an understanding of the New Testament idea of the state of the dead, and the doctrine of future punishment.

It often happens that when an issue is correctly stated, the argument is half completed. At least much useless labor is saved. In the latest discussions of this subject, like the older ones, much time and learning and energy have been expended on false issues, or no issue at all. The learned Dr. Farrar, in his book called *"Eternal Hope,"* betrays weakness in this respect. He finds ample reasons for objecting to the translation of so many original terms by the same English word, Hell, and then, instead of examining critically the original terms, he discusses at length the translation. In this he meets no issue. So also does he confuse the subject, and embarrass himself, by treating incidentals as the main subject.

Take an example. He thus states what he calls "the common view," to which he objects: "These four elements—which make the popular view far darker than that held in the Roman Church, and far darker even than that of St. Augustine—are 1. The physical torments, the material agonies, the '*sapiens ignis,*' of eternal punishment; 2. The supposition of its necessarily endless duration for all who incur it; 3. The opinion that it is thus incurred by the vast mass of mankind, and 4. That it is a doom passed irreversibly at the moment of death on all who die in a state of sin."

Of these "four elements," three are "accretions." They do not form any necessary part of "the common doctrine" of eternal punishment, as taught in the New Testament. The "physical torments," and "material agonies," may be at once eliminated. They are no part of the doctrine. In the discussion of the *nature* of future punishment, they might be considered, if any one should affirm a view that would require it; but in an inquiry concerning the *fact* of eternal punishment, this "element" is out of place. So also is it immaterial to the issue whether the "vast mass of mankind," or only relatively a small portion, shall incur the final doom. It is not a question of numbers, for the fact is equally palpable, and the doctrine just as true, if only a small number are finally lost, as if the vast mass were involved. Nor does it make any difference whether the doom is passed irreversibly at the moment of death, or is morally determined by the accumulations of guilt during life, and judicially announced in the day of judgment. If it ever becomes "irreversible" there must be a moment when the crisis is reached. Whether that be at death, or before, or after, is not the material fact. Thus these "four elements" are reduced to a single point, and that is the fact to be determined by testimony. It is simply a question—the same old question—whether eternal punishment is the possible doom of any portion of the human race.

The time was when, in this discussion, it was necessary to affirm and maintain the fact that there is punishment after death. Now nearly all, if not quite all, who take the Scriptures as authority, admit this fact. Mr. Austin — Universalist — says, "Universalism neither rejects nor adopts the doctrine of future punishment." It leaves its adherents to take such views on this subject as seem the most consistent to them. This prudence saves labor. It narrows down the issue, leaving only the question of finality or duration to be determined. This issue will be met by the application of the word *Gehenna*. It is met by *Hades* only in part. The examination which we propose of these terms will settle the main fact, and lay the foundation for the study of terms which express duration.

Chapter II.

ERRORS ANTAGONIZED.

THE best way to oppose error is to assert the truth. But sometimes duty requires that truth be used aggressively. Indeed, it is agressive in its nature. That particular truth asserted in this treatise opposes divers errors, some of which are popular and deleterious, while others are more speculative and limited.

The first is Universalism. This is an old heresy. It dates back in some form or other to the days of Origen. This Father doubted the eternity of future punishment, and expressed a hope for the restoration or those dying in sin. He was much given to fanciful interpretations of the Scriptures, and pursued metaphorical and spiritual meanings beyond the limits of sober criticism. But his speculations were not generally accepted. Yet a vague line of Restorationism and Destructionism may be traced through the opinions of the Fathers. They were not less curious than men of later times, and sought to penetrate the mysteries of the future with equal earnestness, and often with equal skill and learning. Out of their speculations came the Romish dogma of Purgatory. But no well-defined system of Universalism was developed. This is of modern growth. Its history is instructive, but we can not trace it here.

Under this general head we class all the forms of doctrine that assert the ultimate holiness and happiness of all the race. Formerly Restorationists and Universalists were distinguished by broad lines of difference, having respect to the terms and process of salvation. Now the distinction is unimportant. Nearly all admit suffering after death. And under this head most of the Unitarians are classed. But few believe in eternal punishment. It is possible that some expect the wicked to drop out of existence.

If the Bible authorizes the views herein set forth, then, in some way, somewhere in the universe, the incorrigible of the race will be abandoned of God, and left to suffer forever the results of a life of sin. That somewhere is Hell. At least it is called Hell in our language. Any other name would do as well, if it conveyed the idea. We do not contend about names. If the state were nameless, it would prove as deep and wide and solid and immovable. If any human soul fails forever of the happiness of heaven, Universalism fails in all its forms.

The next error antagonized is the *soul-sleeping* doctrine of Adventists, and other materialists. This theory is old, and has linked itself from time to time with different systems, but in its essential features it is always the same. It denies the essential difference between spirit and matter, and insists that the soul dies with the body, or at least that it so far shares with the body as to lose consciousness. In most cases it is confounded with the body, and is supposed to have no life apart from the body. This is materialism. Of course those who entertain such ideas of the soul have no room for a separate state of souls, except as they may speak thus of the silence and darkness and stillness of the unconscious and non-existent state. And very naturally this class deny consciousness to the wicked in their final abode. Some of them hold that the ungodly die as the beasts that perish, and have no hereafter. Others suppose that the unconsciousness will be broken by the resurrection of soul and body, to be again consigned to the sleep that knows no waking, after the judgment-day. With these theoretical details we have nothing to do. They rest on a false basis; their philosophy is gross and shallow; and they are all at variance with the Scriptures.

If *Hades* be the state of departed souls, there *are* departed souls. It is not a state of nothingness. In it are the consciousness and memory and will and sensibilities of real personalities, disembodied though they be. There, too, is the home of the angels that sinned. Then, if the soul be spiritual—if it survive death—if it carry with it the elements of character gained on earth, then the invisible world is a world of activity, of emotion, of joy, and of pain and of despair. The world which the Bible calls *Hades* is as real as this, and immeasurably vaster in all that is good and great in its heavenward aspects, and all that is dark and ruinous in the surroundings of the unsaved. It is a world of spirits, where the pure share the delights of heaven, and the impure bewail the follies of the past, and dread the deepening shadows of the unpromising future.

It is an intermediate state. Intermediate, not necessarily as between earth and heaven, in the sense of locality or place or space, but in the sense of time between death and the resurrection. The good reach not their highest destiny till they rise in the "resurrection of the just," and "put on immortality" with respect to the "mortal" part that returned to dust. And the wicked will not reach their final doom till they "come forth unto the resurrection of damnation." The unjust are "reserved unto the day of judgment to be punished." Canon Farrar thought that the doctrine of an intermediate state would mitigate the rigidity of the common conception of future punishment, but seems not to have been able to find a place for it without resorting to the mediæval notion of place, and admitting the essential thought of a Romish purgatory. It is, however, in harmony with the New Testament idea of *Hades* that we hold to an intermediate state, in which character is fixed and destiny certain, with no purifying element in the flames of lust and hate with which the ungodly are tormented. It is neither limbus nor purgatory; nor is it the highest heaven or the deepest hell. So far as locality is concerned, the good are in paradise, and this the apostle called the "third heaven." The redeemed from earth, even before the resurrection are "before the throne of God, and serve him day and night in his temple."

Another prevalent error, antagonized by the Scriptural doctrine of *Hades* and *Gehenna*, is found in connection with modern speculations concerning the resurrection of the dead. For the want of a better descriptive term, we may designate the particular view of the resurrection to which we allude, the *progressive theory*. It rejects the notion that the body shall rise, and assumes that the resurrection state is gained immediately after death. Of course, it has no room for an intermediate state.

This progressive theory of the resurrection owes its origin in its modern form to the dreamy philosophy of Swedenborg. It was formulated by him and his admirers, and vigorously set forth and advocated by Professor Bush, some thirty years ago, and since then has found much favor with theologians of different schools, and has been accepted as an important part of diverse systems of doctrine. Its influence is felt in the Evangelical Churches, as well as in others. Universalists and Unitarians, of different shades of opinion in regard to spiritual truths, very generally fall in with this theory of the resurrection. It is, therefore, sufficiently formidable to deserve the notice we give it.

Let us state it more definitely. It assumes that man is possessed of a compound nature; that this nature consists of body, soul, and spirit; that the body is material, earthy, sensual; that the soul is spiritual, ethereal, immortal; that the spirit is pure spirit, incorruptible and, of course, immortal. All this sounds well, and is plausible to philosophical minds, while it apparently harmonizes with the language of Scripture. No error is so dangerous as that which sounds and looks like the truth. But we must look again. This theory assumes that the spirit is the substratum of being, the essence of personality, the real ego or selfhood of the man; that the soul, the seat of sensations and emotions, is the vesture or inner casement of the spirit; and that the body is the outer casement, or the vehicle or tabernacle of the soul, and the link of connection with the material world. It assumes, furthermore, that death cuts the link that binds man to earth and to material things, dissolves the tabernacle and consigns it to its original dust, where it abides, without hope of rising again, while the soul emerges from its confinement in the house of clay, and develops into the full character of the resurrection or spiritual body, in which the spirit resides forever. Accordingly, the body has no share in the rising again, and the resurrection occurs immediately at the hour of death, and as soon as the spiritual body frees itself from the impurities and evil tendencies contracted in the body, the full blessedness of the resurrection state is attained. As a theory, this is all beautiful;

but it is not found in the Scriptures; it has no place for the second coming of Christ, for the general judgment, for an intermediate state, for a simultaneous rising again, or for the redemption of our bodies. Its assumptions in regard to soul and spirit are unsound. It is fatally lacking in philosophy and Scripture warrant, and we therefore present it as one of the subtle heresies antagonized by the teachings of our Lord with reference to *Hades* and *Gehenna*.

There are some errors prevalent in the Church, in regard to the use and application of these terms, which are not classed with heresies, but are held, or rather entertained, by orthodox believers in future punishment, and which confuse the mind and weaken the arguments in support of right conclusions, and therefore ought to be corrected. These, however, will appear and find correction in the course of the argument, but to indicate them here may shorten the work and facilitate the result.

It is popularly supposed that *Gehenna* is part of *Hades*, and that the wicked enter it when they enter *Hades*. The opposite of this has been stated, and will be maintained. There is no passage that requires such a belief, while the whole current of testimony is against it. And yet the entire force of argument against the doctrine of Hell is directed against this erroneous view. The simple correction of it destroys a great portion of the opposing arguments, and especially those which assume the form of criticism in connection with the original terms. *Hades* is before the resurrection, and *Gehenna* is after that consummation.

The doctrine of Hell carries with it the idea of the existence of fallen angels as its inhabitants. These are the devils. They were once good, as all created beings were created good, but they fell under the leadership of a chief, revealed to us as Beelzebub, the prince of the devils. The popular notion is that their original home was in heaven—the heaven to which we aspire, which is the home of God, and the abode of holy angels and the redeemed from earth. This popular notion is not well founded. It overlooks important facts. The law of the universe appears to be that all intelligent, responsible beings, destined to the development of moral character as the basis of moral condition, should have their first existence on probation. The probation of man is not an exception but the rule of the divine government over the moral creation. In harmony with this the angels were first placed on trial, somewhere in the wide domain of the Almighty. Some of them kept the law of their probation, were confirmed in holiness, and ascended to the home and companionship of God, and are now the "holy angels." Others of them "kept not their first estate," but "left their own habitation," and violated the law of their probation, and, under the leadership of Satan, fell into condemnation. These are now "the angels that sinned," "reserved under chains of darkness unto judgment." Where "their own habitation" was, is not revealed. It was somewhere in the universe, and, in the symbolical language of the Book of Revelation, the word "heaven" will include it, though it was not the heaven of heavens, where sin never enters, where the good abide, forever free from the possibility of defection. These angels that sinned are in *Tartarus*. This is another word for that portion of *Hades*, or for that state in the invisible world, where the unholy abide. It is not so general a word as *Hades*, nor is it at all like *Gehenna*. It belongs to *Hades*, but it has no connection with *Gehenna*.

Another misapprehension on this subject is, that the devil and his angels are in the final Hell of the lost, the "lake of fire." *Gehenna*. We have already intimated that this can not be other than a misapprehension. The devils are yet in *Tartarus*. This is in *Hades*, or coexistent with *Hades*. It is on this side of the period of the resurrection, and therefore this side of the judgment-day. But it is at the judgment that the devils, with the unsaved of earth, will be cast into the "everlasting fire"—*Gehenna*. No one enters there until judicially assigned to it at the judgment-day. Then when the "devil and his angels" reach the "lake of fire," they will tempt the people of God no more. Their access to earth will be over.

But now they have access to mortals. Here is their field of action. When cast out of that "heaven" which was "their own habitation," they were cast out "into the earth." They are in the invisible world, yet they are here. The visible and invisible worlds are not wide apart. They lie in close proximity. We can not trace the line between them. We can not lift the veil that separates them. Darkness covers the earth. Invisibility is all around us. If our eyes were opened we might see the mountains and hills covered with the chariots of God. The invisible laps and interlaps with the visible; the two worlds trench, but do not blend; they touch, attract, repel, impress, and move on together, as matter and spirit can, yet they remain distinct. Here then is the war of spiritual forces. Here is the theater of Satan's activity, and here is the seat of his empire. The lordship of this world is the prize for which he contends. Here are gathered all the spiritual forces of sin that the universe contains. And this is the reason the incarnation was here. Christ came into the heart of the kingdom of Satan, met him in the citadal of his power, grappled him in the domain of death, and wrenched from his grasp the keys of *Hades*. "For this purpose the Son of God was manifested, that he might destroy the works of the devil."

But this chapter is to state errors and misconceptions of the truth, not to refute them. The refutation is the result to be reached. The preliminary statement is to aid in the application of the argument, as we proceed, and to forestall objections that lie only against incorrect presentations of the doctrine advocated. The next chapter will deal with authorities, and is given because there are so many who are timid about accepting any doctrinal position that is not supported by the influence of great names.

Chapter III.

HADES—AUTHORITIES.

AS already said, the meaning of the word *Hades* is not in dispute. It means the invisible world, the dwelling place of souls. All classes of religionists agree to this.

The origin of the word may not be traced with absolute certainty, nor is it important that it should be. In Homer's time it was a name, and seems to have designated a person or divinity whose special dominion was in the under world, which is unseen. But upon this point it will be sufficient to cite the following from Smith's "Classical Dictionary:"

"*Hades*, or Pluto, the god of the nether world. Plato observes that people preferred calling him Pluto (the giver of wealth) to pronouncing the dreaded name of Hades. Hence we find that in ordinary life and in the mysteries the name Pluto became generally established, while the poets preferred the ancient name Hades or the form Pleuteus. The Roman poets use the names Dis, Orcus, and Tartarus as synonymous with Pluto, or the god of the nether world. *Hades* was the son of Saturn and Rhea, and brother of Jupiter and Neptune. . . . In the division of the world among the three brothers, Hades (Pluto) obtained the nether world, the abode of the shades, over which he ruled. Hence he is called the infernal Jupiter, or the king of the shades. He possessed a helmet which rendered the wearer invisible. . . . He kept the gates of the lower world closed, that no shades might be able to escape or return to the regions of light. . . . Being the king of the lower world, Pluto is the giver of all the blessings that come from the earth; he is the possessor and giver of all the metals contained in the earth, and hence his name Pluto. He bears several surnames referring to his ultimately assembling all mortals in his kingdom. . . . His ordinary attributes are the key of *Hades* and *Cerberus*. . . . In Homer *Hades* is invariably the name of the god; but in later times it was transferred to his house, his abode or kingdom, so that it became a name of the nether world."

To this we add from Anthon's "Classic Dictionary" the following: "*Hades*, the place of departed spirits, according to Grecian mythology, from *a, not,* and *eido, to see*, as denoting the lower or invisible world. Its divisions were Elysium and Tartarus, the respective abodes of good and bad. In Homeric times, however, this arrangement formed no part of the popular creed. The earliest beliefs did not separate the invisible world into apartments, but represented the souls of the dead as pursuing much the same employments, and showing the same passions and characteristics, as on earth. It was in the later developments of thought that the world of spirits was divided into the higher and lower abodes, for the good and bad, and this later conception prevailed among the Hebrews as well as the Greeks and Romans, and formed the staple belief down to the time of the advent of Christ."

The following from "M'Clintock and Strong's Cyclopædia," is in harmony with the foregoing: "*Hades*, a Greek word (derived according to the best established and most generally received etymology, from privative *a*, and *idien*) means strictly *what is out of sight*, or possibly, if applied to a person, *what puts out of sight*. In earlier Greek this last was, if not its only, at least its prevailing application; in Homer it occurs only as the personal designation of Pluto, the lord of the invisible world, and who was probably so designated, not from being himself invisible—for that belonged to him in common with the heathen gods generally—but from his power to render mortals invisible, the invisible-making deity. The Greeks, however, in process of time, abandoned this use of *Hades*, and when the Greek Scriptures were written the word was scarcely ever applied except to the place of the departed. In the classical writers, therefore, it is used to denote *Orcus*, or the infernal regions. In the Greek version of the Old Testament it is the common rendering for the Hebrew *Sheôl*, though in the form there often appears a remnant of the original personified application; for example, in Genesis xxxvii, 35, "I will go down to my son *eis hadou*, that is, into the abodes or house of *Hades* (*domous* or *oikon* being understood). This elliptical form was common both in the classics and in Scripture, even after *Hades* was never thought of but as a region or place of abode."

Perhaps as clear and satisfactory a description of *Hades* and *Gehenna*, and especially of the difference between them, as can be found in the language, is in Dr. George Campbell's Dissertations, in which all that is said above is corroborated, and the general positions of this book, with perhaps a single exception, are sustained. Of *Hades*, Dr. Campbell says, "The corresponding word in the Old Testament is *Sheôl*, which signifies the state of the dead in general, without regard to the goodness or badness of the persons, their happiness or misery. In translating the word the LXX have almost invariably used *Hades*." After verifying and illustrating this general statement, he adds: "So much then for the literal sense of the word *Hades*, which, as has been observed, implies neither *hell* nor *grave;* but the place or state of departed souls." (Diss. pp. 180–191.)

In William Smith's "Comprehensive Dictionary of the Bible" we read: "The ancient Greeks and Hebrews seem to have agreed in representing *Hades* or *Sheôl* as (1.) the *common* receptacle of departed spirits, good and bad; (2.) divided into two compartments, the one an Elysium or abode of bliss for the good, the other a *Tartarus*, or abode of sorrow and punishment for the wicked; (3.) situated under ground, in the mid regions of the earth. But while the heathen had no prospect beyond its shadowy realms, the believing Hebrew regarded *Sheôl* as only his temporary and intermediate abode. In the New Testament, *Hades*, like *Sheôl*, sometimes merely equals the *grave* (Rev. xx, 13; Acts ii, 31; 1 Cor. xv, 55); or in general *the unseen world*. It is in this sense that the creeds say of our lord 'He went down into Hell,' meaning the state of the dead in general, without any restriction of happiness or misery, a doctrine certainly, though only virtually, expressed in Scripture (Eph. iv, 9; Acts ii, 25–31). Elsewhere in the New Testament *Hades* is used of a place of torment. (Luke xvi, 23; Matt, xi, 23, etc.) Consequently it has been the prevalent, almost the universal, notion that *Hades* is an *intermediate* state, between death and the resurrection, divided into two parts, one the abode of the blessed and the other of the lost. The expression most frequently used in the New Testament for the place of future punishment is *Gehenna* or *Gehenna of fire.*"

The only dissent from this that needs to be mentioned, is the fact that *Hades*, in the New Testament, never means the grave, and should never be taken as relating in any way to the dead body. We might quote authorities similar to the above indefinitely, including lexicographers, critics, commentators, historians, and theologians of all classes and of all schools of belief; for it is remarkable that, after all that has been said and written in the advocacy of so many conflicting views of the state of the dead, there is scarcely any difference anywhere discoverable among men whose opinions are of any weight in regard to the meaning of this word. We might therefore close this chapter, and proceed to the New Testament use of *Hades*, but, for the satisfaction of those who do not have access to many books, a few more brief citations will be given.

Trench on the Parables, in expounding the case of the rich man and Lazarus, gives the following: "In Hell, or *in Hades* rather; for as Abraham's bosom is not heaven, though it will issue in heaven, so neither is *Hades* hell, though to issue in it, when cast with death into the lake of fire, which is the proper hell. It is the place of painful restraint, where the souls of the wicked are reserved to the judgment of the great day; it is 'the deep,' whither the devils prayed that they might not be sent to be tormented before the time," etc.

Dr. Knapp says, "This place was denominated by the Hebrews *Sheôl*—by the Greeks *Hades*, the word by which the LXX always translate *Sheôl*. Neither of these is used in the Scriptures to signify exactly the grave, still less, the place of the damned; nor are they used in this sense by any of the Fathers in the first three centuries." The word was applied by the Fathers, according to its proper meaning, neither to the receptacle of the dead body nor to the final state of the lost, but to the state of the soul this side of the resurrection of the dead. It was this use of the word that gave rise to the abuse that began to show itself, perhaps earlier than the close of the third century, in connection with the intermediate state, and resulted in the Romish invention of the Limbus, wherein those unfitted for heaven or hell, were supposed to be detained till purified. Purgatory, as now held by Romanists, is but the growth and development of this fanciful notion of the Fathers, and has no foundation whatever in the right use of *Hades*, as found in the Scriptures.

Universalist writers of respectability hesitate not a moment in agreeing with the statements above given. Some of them have inclined to give the word the meaning of *grave*, as *Sheôl* is so rendered in the Old Testament, and as *Hades* is so translated once in the New Testament; but the attempt to so interpret it is now nearly, if not wholly, abandoned. Indeed it is doubted that one can be found who will contend for the word *grave* as an equivalent of *Hades*. The testimony in favor of the application to the state of the soul after death is overwhelming, so that there is in reality no other side to the subject. Ballou, Balfour, Pingree, Thomas, Rogers, Austin, Thayer, Gurley, Weaver, Nye, Williamson—in short, all who have shaped the system in this country, and brought it to its present standing, concur in applying *Hades* to the state of the dead in general, and calling it the unseen world.

Canon Farrar, whose recent utterances on the subject of a possible probation after death have produced so much astonishment on one hand, and gratification on the other, and who is, in consequence, in such high esteem by all "liberalists," does not venture upon any definition of this word contrary to that herein presented and maintained. In his prefatory dissertation he says: "One of the three words rendered 'hell' occurs but once, in 2 Peter, ii, 4. It is the Greek *Tartarus*, and ought to be so rendered. It can not be rendered 'hell,' for it refers to an intermediate state previous to judgment. Another is *Hades*, which is the exact equivalent of the Hebrew *Sheôl*, as a place for both the bad and the Good. (Acts ii, 27–36.) It tells directly against the received notion of 'hell,' because (like Tartarus in 2 Peter, ii, 4) it means an intermediate state of the soul previous to judgment." (Preface to "Eternal Hope.")

The learned doctor, though prompt to assume that this word "tells directly against the received notion of hell"—by which *he* refers to a final state of "material torture"—gives correct definitions, and also recognizes the important fact of a "judgment" after the intermediate state. We make no issue with him here, but commend this particular view of the subject to the consideration of his cordial admirers, who may be so taken up with his glittering rhetoric as to overlook the logical bearing of this fatal concession.

The following summary of the ancient notions on this subject by Dr. J. M. Good, will be in place here. After speaking of the doctrine of the Platonists and others who had imbibed the idea of ultimate absorption into the Deity, he says: "While such were the philosophical traditions, the popular tradition appears to have been of a different kind, and as much more ancient as it was more extensive. It taught that the disembodied spirit became a ghost as soon as it separated from the corporeal frame; a thin, misty, aerial form, somewhat larger than life, with feeble voice, shadowy limbs; knowledge superior to what was possessed while in the flesh; capable, under particular circumstances, of rendering itself visible; and retaining so much of its former features as to be recognized upon its apparition; in a few instances wandering about for a certain period of time after death, but for the most part conveyed to a common receptacle situated in the interior of the earth, and denominated *Sheôl*, *Hades*, or the world of shades. Such was the general belief of the multitude in almost all countries from a very early period of time; with this difference, that the *Hades* of various nations was supposed to exist in some remote situation on the surface of the earth, and that of others in the clouds. . . . In many parts of the world, though not in all, this common tradition of the people was carried much farther, and, under different modifications, made to develop a very important and correct doctrine; for it was believed in most countries, that this hell, *Hades*, or invisible world, is divided into two very distinct and opposite regions by a broad and impassable gulf; that the one is a seat of happiness, a paradise, or Elysium, and the other a seat of misery, a Gehenna or Tartarus; and that there is a supreme magistrate and an impartial tribunal belonging to the infernal shades, before which the ghost must appear, and by which he is sentenced to the one or the other, according to the deeds done in the body."

As this was the popular belief among nearly all nations long before the coming of Christ, and as it accords so nearly with the teachings of the Hebrew prophets, and with the prevalent notions of the Jews in the Messiah's own time, and was not contradicted but rather corroborated by him in his parables, in its main features, we must conclude with the learned Doctor quoted above that though found in the earliest records of Egyptian history, it was not invented by them, but "had a higher origin, and that it constituted a part of the patriarchal or antediluvian creed, retained in a few channels, though forgotten or obliterated in others; and consequently, that it was a divine communication in a very early age."

Bishop Pierson, on the creed, says that

Hades was used among the ancient Greeks as comprehending all the souls both of the wicked and the just; hence they did send the best men to *Hades*, there to be happy, and taught rewards to be received there as well as punishments."

Dr. Alex. M'Leod tells us that "it is a general term for the place of departed spirits: as if we should say, such a one is gone to the invisible world; he is dead; he is gone to the world of spirits."

Dr. Samuel Clarke says: "Whenever the place of torment is spoken of, the word hell in the original is always Gehenna; but whenever the state of the dead, in general, is intended, it is always expressed by a different word, *Hades*, which though we render by the same word, hell, yet its signification is, at large, the invisible state."

Dr. A. Clarke says: "*Hades*, the place of separate spirits. The sea and death have the bodies of all human beings; *Hades* has their spirits."

Dr. Lange's "Commentary on Luke xvi, says: "*Hades* is the general designation of departed spirits."

Dr. Hodge says of *Hades* and the English word hell: "Both mean the unseen world. The one signifies what is unseen, the other what is covered and thus hidden from view. . . . In Scriptural language, therefore, to descend into *Hades* or hell, means nothing more than to descend to the grave, to pass from the visible into the invisible world, as happens to all men when they die and are buried."

Mr. J. Wesley says, of the rich man: "In *Hades*; that is, in the unseen or invisible world. It must be observed that both the rich man and Lazarus were in Hades, though in different regions of it."

Dr. Whedon, on the same passage, says: "In hell, or *Hades*, or the great unseen; that is the invisible place, or region of disembodied spirits."

Bishop Beveridge, in his "Exposition of the Thirty-nine Articles," says: "Though therefore we can not but acknowledge that the Greek word *Hades* may sometimes, both in Scripture and other writings, signify no more than the receptacle of souls in general, as the grave is the receptacle of the bodies;

yet it can not be denied but that it often, if not mostly, is used to express the receptacle of sinful souls in particular, or that which we in English call Hell, the place of the damned." This eminent writer affirms that the ancient poets often used *Hades* to signify the other world in general, even in as large a sense as *thanatos*, for which it was often employed, and in attestation he cites examples from Homer, Sophocles,· Pindar, and Theognis; and this, too, while he was contending for its restricted sense, where it was used with reference to the soul of Christ, which descended into it but was not left there.

Numberless quotations might be made to the same effect, but these will suffice. They have not been selected at random, but with reference to variety. Their voice is the echo of all Christian·learning. We therefore proceed with confidence, not to establish something new, but to use and apply this old truth, which is sustained by the uniform testimony of Romanist and Protestant, Orthodox and Liberalist. The only new point we insist upon is the entire separation of *Gehenna* from *Hades*, and this is amply justified by the authorities of all schools and all Churches, as well as by the necessity of the case. We now turn to the final authority, the New Testament.

Chapter IV.

HADES—SCRIPTURE USE.

AFTER all the light the authorities afford in regard to this word, the ordinary reader of the Scriptures will desire to see these testimonies verified by an examination of the several passages in which the word is found. We therefore proceed to a brief glance at each occurrence of *Hades* in the New Testament, dwelling only so long as is necessary to gather the idea of the text in its bearing on the subject in hand.

As before said, this word is used eleven times in the New Testament. But in several instances it is duplicated or repeated in the same connection, so that in reality it is found in only eight passages. These are in the Gospels, the Acts, the Epistles, and Revelation. In some places the language is figurative, and in others the word is to be taken in its most literal sense. In all cases, however, its real meaning is easily traced, and its application to the invisible world of spirits, and not to the ultimate condition of the lost, is readily seen.

It is first used, somewhat figuratively, with reference to Capernaum, both by Matthew and Luke. "And thou, Capernaum, which art exalted unto heaven, shalt be brought down to *Hades;* for if the mighty works which have been done in thee, had been done in Sodom, it would have remained until this day." (Matt. xi, 23.) "And thou Capernaum, which art exalted to heaven, shalt be thrust down to *Hades.*" (Luke x, 15.) The discourse is the same, recorded by the two evangelists. Capernaum was the most favored place in the world, by reason of the fact that our Savior made it his home the greater part of the time during his public ministry in Galilee. Here he taught and wrought as nowhere else. And yet he foresaw the coming desolation, and warned the inhabitants of their coming degradation. "Thou shalt be brought down to *Hades"*—to the state of the dead. If there is any passage where *Hades* is used metaphorically for earthly desolations, this is the one; yet here the sense is retained. The dead are popularly considered deprived of all privileges. To be cast down from so great a height to so great a depth was an extreme judgment. The word is here used for the opposite of heaven. In the popular conception it signified the state of the dead, and therefore the very lowest possible condition; so that this metaphorical use did not mislead, though it does not exhaust the meaning of the word. The sense it yields is good, if taken wholly in the figurative sense; for the desolation did come, so that for many years it has scarcely been possible to identify the place where this once favored little city stood. And if we look beyond the figurative use of the word, to see the ground of the metaphor in its literal meaning, the point is well sustained. It is the under world, the invisible state, the state of disembodied souls. The use of such a word to denote the desolation of the city, gave a striking picture of the utter ruin awaiting the people, besides suggesting that their final accountability would be revealed in the invisible world rather than in this world. Altogether the passage is in the strictest harmony with the sense we claim for this word, although its use here would go but a little way towards fixing its real meaning, if this were the only passage containing it.

It is next found in the following very familiar passage: "And I say also unto thee, that thou art Peter, and upon this rock I will build my Church, and the gates of *Hades* shall not prevail against it." (Matt. xvi, 18.) The idea is, that the Church of Christ is built upon so strong a foundation, and so well guarded, that all the powers of the unseen world can not successfully oppose it. "The *gates* of *Hades*" may be taken as the passage-way to the unseen state; that is, death. Through death we enter the invisible world. Then the sense is that the Church shall not be destroyed by the death of all its members. As some die others will take their places, and thus perpetuate the Church through all the ages. But this is the lowest and most literal sense of the words, and by no means expresses their force. The Church is a citadel, founded upon a rock, withstanding siege and assault. The word "gates" denotes powers, as the strongest attacks are upon the gates, and the sudden sorties and dashes upon the enemies' lines issue from the "gates." So, also, it means devices, skill, strategy, as in olden times the judges and counselors sat in the gates and planned for war and for peace. The force and cunning of the enemy are expressed by the metaphor of the "gates." The leader in this war upon the Church is Satan. His home is in the invisible world. His army is composed of the angels that sinned. He reaches the Church, in his fiercest assaults, through the agency of the unbelieving and irreligious of this world. He commands the forces of ignorance and learning, of science and superstition, and uses the high and the low, the refined and the vulgar, as the occasion requires. But all his malice and cunning, and all his experience and power, will be employed in vain. "The gates of *Hades* shall not prevail." The citadel will never be carried. *Hades* has its ordinary meaning here, its popular meaning as the invisible world of darkness. It is co-existent with the Church in this world. From it issue the forces that give the Church its sorest trials.

The next passage is more expressive. It is the case of the rich man. Luke xvi, 23: "The rich man also died, and was buried; and in *Hades* he lifted up his eyes, being in torments," etc. This will be fully considered in a subsequent chapter. For the present it is enough to look at the relation in which the word stands to death. The rich man first died; he died literally, and was buried; and then he was found in *Hades*, the state of the dead. This is natural. There is no sort of difficulty in accepting the statement in the literal sense. The man died and was immediately in *Hades*. The body was buried, and the soul, the real man, was in the disembodied state.

Whether this be parable or not does not affect the sense of this word. In any view we take of the events described, the representation is made of two men dying, and of one it is said that after death he lifted up his eyes in *Hades*, being in torment. The representation is true to fact, or it is false and misleading. The latter can not, therefore the former must, be admitted. The representation is true to fact. Men die, and after death appear in *Hades*, the invisible world. They appear at once, without delay, and in a conscious state, so as to be "comforted" or "tormented," according to condition. This is fact, not fiction. And thus far it settles the meaning of the word. It settles it by higher authority than lexicons or commentaries, by the last arbiter of words—use; and by use that can not be wrong, for it is in the discourse of our Lord himself.

We next find the word used in the Acts of the Apostles, and so as to confirm the foregoing and shed further light. The language is Peter's; the occasion, the Pentecost; the subject, the resurrection of Christ; the words, a quotation from the sixteenth Psalm, with comments: "Therefore did my heart rejoice, and my tongue was glad; moreover also my flesh shall rest in hope, because thou wilt not leave my soul in *Hades*, neither wilt thou suffer thine Holy One to see corruption. Thou hast made known to me the ways of life; thou shalt make full of joy with thy countenance." Thus far the quotation;

now the comment: "Men and brethren, let me freely speak unto you of the patriarch David, that he is both dead and buried, and his sepulcher is with us unto this day. Therefore being a prophet, and knowing that God had sworn with an oath to him, that of the fruit of his loins, according to the flesh, he would raise up Christ to sit on his throne: he, seeing this before, spake of the resurrection of Christ, that his soul was not left in *Hades*, neither his flesh did see corruption." Acts ii, 26–31.

The resurrection of Christ consisted of two distinct facts—the coming back of the soul from *Hades*, and the escape of the body from the power of death. Here begins the association of *death* and *Hades*, which, as we advance, we shall find uninterrupted, and very significant. It recognizes the dual nature of man, and the separation that death produces, and that continues till the resurrection of the dead. Death takes the body, and turns it over to corruption; and *Hades* receives the soul, and holds it as long as it is separated from the body. This proves all we affirm.

It shows that *Hades* is the receptacle of disembodied souls; that they enter it at once, and abide there till the resurrection; and that they leave it in the resurrection, while the body escapes the dominion of death. Thus Christ arose. His soul came back from *Hades*, and his body came back from death before it saw corruption. And this is the pattern of our resurrection. Who, then, can doubt that the body participates?

This Scripture is the warrant for the assertion in the Apostles' Creed, which has occasioned so much discussion, that Christ "descended into hell." The trouble is with the English word. His soul entered *Hades*, yet not in the sense of going into the abode of the lost. On the day he died he entered "paradise," the place of the pure and the good. It was the invisible world,—the separate state of souls,—where the body did not go. *Hades*, in its broadest and truest sense, includes paradise, as well as the abode of the condemned. It includes the spirits of just men made perfect, the countless millions of the redeemed before the throne of God, as well as the myriads that sink in darkness, and cry with the rich man, "for I am tormented in this flame."

We now turn to 1 Cor. xv, 55: "O death, where is thy sting? O *Hades*, where is thy victory?" Here only is *Hades* translated "grave"—a rendering that should never occur, for the reason that *Hades* is the receptacle of the soul, not of the body. The passage is an application of the sentiment in Hosea xiii, 14: "O death, I will be thy plagues; O *Hades*, I will be thy destruction." It is not a quotation nor a translation, but an application, and an application in Paul's words. The subject was the resurrection, which delivers the body from death and the soul from *Hades*. Death had held possession of the body, and the resurrection had just rescued it, in the consummation which the Apostle described; hence his triumphant exclamation, "O death, where is thy sting?" *Hades* had held possession of the soul until the same blessed triumph; hence the exclamation, "O *Hades*, where is thy victory?" Death and *Hades* are joined together in their dominion and in their destruction. This fact is worthy of note. It means that the resurrection affects both. It takes the soul out of the separate state and the body out of the power of death. The resurrection is of the whole person, but not as held by those who expect the soul to repose in death with the body. Paul was not a materialist of that kind; nor was he such a spiritualist as to exclude the body from any share in the resurrection. He believed in the destruction of death. There could be no resurrection without it. Death must be swallowed up in victory. The mortal must put on immortality. And this in a moment, in the twinkling of an eye, at the last trump. It is not at the moment of death, but at the moment of the destruction of death. It is not when the soul enters *Hades*, but when it leaves *Hades*. The crowning act of the Redeeming power of our Lord Jesus Christ is the destruction of death and *Hades*.

In the next passage containing *Hades*, we find it in like manner joined with death, as it is indeed in all the passages yet to be considered: "I am he that liveth, and was dead; and, behold I am alive for evermore, Amen;

and have the keys of *Hades* and of death."
(Rev. i, 18.) This is the victorious language
of Christ, after his resurrection. The "keys"
are symbols of authority. The possession
of them by the risen Lord denotes the fact
that he had the power and the right to un-
lock the gates of death and *Hades*, and release
whom he would and when he would. He is
the Lord of the unseen world, and the con-
queror of the king of terrors: "For to this end
Christ both died and rose and revived, that
he might be Lord both of the dead and living." Through death he gained the power to
destroy him who had the power of death.
His own resurrection proves his power to
raise the dead, and is the standing pledge
that, in the day of his second coming, he will
deliver the bodies of men from death, as his
own body was delivered, and their souls from
Hades, as his own soul came back from the
disembodied state. As surely, then, as death
and *Hades* are affected by the resurrection,
so surely will the soul and body share the
rising. The resurrection is a miracle. It
must be studied in the light of miracles, and
not in the light of science. It depends on

the power of God, and not on the laws of nature. The proof is in the living again of him who was dead, and who holds the keys of death and of *Hades.*

The next passage is highly figurative. Both *death* and *Hades* are personified, but the association is kept up, and the natural order maintained: "And I looked, and behold a pale horse: and his name that sat on him was Death, and Hades followed with him." (Rev. vi, 8.) Death is a warrior, going forth to conquest, and *Hades* is his inseparable companion. This is true to fact. Death advances and strikes down the body, and *Hades* follows and receives the soul. Each has his work. This companionship is not merely rhetorical, nor is it accidental. It is one of the divinely ordered facts of revelation, standing as a guide to our inquiries in relation to the mysteries of our being and our destiny.

We come now to the last instance of the use of this word in the Holy Scriptures, and the passage confirms all we have said, and gives emphasis to the thought that the resurrection destroys both death and *Hades.*

"And I saw a great white throne, and him that sat on it, from whose face the earth and heaven fled away; and there was found no place for them. And I saw the dead, small and great, stand before God; and the books were opened; and another book was opened, which is the book of life: and the dead were judged out of those things which were written in the books, according to their works. And the sea gave up the dead which were in it; and *death* and *Hades* delivered up the dead which were in them: and they were judged every man according to their works. And *death* and *Hades* were cast into the lake of fire. This is the second death. And whosoever was not found written in the book of life was cast into the lake of fire." (Rev. xx, 11-15.)

The first aim in studying this passage should be to fix its chronological relation. It marks the close of the Gospel dispensation. The seals have all been opened, the vials have all been poured out, the trumpets have all sounded; every symbol marking the epochs of time is past, and the end of the dispensation is come. The symbolic thousand years of Christ's reign is over. Satan has been imprisoned; he has again been loosed, and deceived the nations, and led them in their last conflict, and is now cast into his final doom, the lake of fire. It is the end of time, the end of probation, the end of the world. The passing away of heaven and earth is the last of this mundane sphere. It is the final conflagration when the elements melt with fervent heat.

The next thing is to mark the order of events. The first is the appearance of the "great white throne." This is the coming of the Lord in glory. The second is the delivering up of the dead, which is the resurrection. They come from all the receptacles of human dust, whether earth or sea. Death delivers up their bodies, and *Hades* delivers up their souls. This is the general resurrection. Death retains no victim, and *Hades* retains no human soul. The third event is the judgment. This is the final revelation of the divine righteousness, the formal judicial announcement of destiny. It reaches the entire race. From it there is no appeal. The last point is the execution of the sentence. All the unsaved are cast into the lake of fire. This is "the second death." Death and *Hades*, having completed their reign over the bodies and souls of men, are abolished. The "second death" is not of this nature. So far as we know or can learn, it does not separate soul and body. The beast, the false prophet, the devil, and all not written in the book of life, are cast into the lake of fire. This is the end. Naught remains but the final abode of the saved and lost.

We have now seen the entire use of this word in the New Testament. The conclusion is inevitable. It means the disembodied state between death and the resurrection. It never applies to any state or condition beyond the resurrection. When this fact is apprehended, the way is open for the study of the doctrine of future punishment on its merits. All classes agree that *Hades* does not last forever. It does not mean the place of eternal punishment. It is not the right word for Hell, according to the accepted sense of that word. Hence the destruction of *Hades* is not the destruction of Hell; the coming out of *Hades* is not salvation. The lake of fire is not in *Hades*, nor is it a symbol of *Hades*, nor does it in any wise represent the puishment that is found in *Hades*. The transition from *Hades* to the "lake of fire" is distinctly noted. On the fact of that *transition* hinges the truth or falsity of the doctrine, in very large degree. But this fact itself does not depend on this single passage, positive as it is. The antecedent and accompanying facts which point to that transition are numerous and well sustained. The argument is cumulative and irrefragable.

But, having found that *Hades* is the Scriptural term for the intermediate or disembodied state, without regard to locality or moral condition, and that it can have no substantial meaning unless the soul actually exists apart from the body, a chapter will be devoted to the consideration of the separate existence of the soul, as taught in the Scriptures, without the use of the word *Hades* which implies it.

CHAPTER V.

THE SEPARATE EXISTENCE OF THE SOUL.

IT seems impossible that any one endowed with the consciousness and sensibilities common to our race, and capable of observing the developments of life incident to our history in this world and departure out of it, should live long without asking the question, "If a man die shall he live again?" But, while every one finds something within himself prompting him to ask this question, no one, not aided by revelation, has been able to answer it satisfactorily to himself. The Bible alone has drawn aside the veil which separates eternity from time, so as to reveal to us the fact and the character of the existence of the soul when dislodged from the earthly tabernacle.

But even the Bible does not disclose the mode and surroundings of the life beyond in such a way as to meet all the requirements of curiosity. It does not tell us all about the nature of the separate life, the locality of the abode of the soul, and the pursuits and activities which pertain to it in the invisible world. Many questions arise touching these things which no man can answer, even with the helps of revelation at hand. The design of revelation is not to gratify curiosity, but to command our faith. In harmony with this design, "life and immortality are brought to light." The momentous fact of life eternal as the gift of God through Jesus Christ, is set before us with such impressiveness of language and imagery as to cut off excuse if we live in doubt. But, while this is true in regard to the final state, there is comparatively little said of the particular period of the soul's existence between death and the resurrection. And yet we are not left in utter darkness with reference to this point. The Scriptural idea of the soul's continued existence, and the allusions, direct and indirect, to this period which we denominate the intermediate state, are plain enough, when rightly considered, to assure us that death does not consign us to unconsciousness.

It is proper here to glance at some passages which relate to the continued existence of the soul, and which can not be otherwise construed without great violence: "And fear not them which kill the body, but are not able to kill the soul; but rather fear him which is able to destroy both soul and body in hell." A parallel passage reads, "Be not afraid of them that kill the body, and after that have no more that they can do. But I will forewarn you whom ye shall fear. Fear him, which after he hath killed, hath power to cast into hell." The single point here to be noted is, that the soul is not "killed" when the body is killed. This fact lies upon the surface of the passages, and will not be affected by the most critical prying into the profoundest depths of their meaning. Men may kill the body, but they can not kill the soul. This strikes away the foundation of materialistic conceptions of the soul, as dependent on the bodily organism, and clearly marks its survival of the shock that prostrates the body to the dust. If the passages mean any thing, they mean that the soul is not dependent on the body for its existence; that it is not identical with the body; that it is not a part of the body; that it does not die with the body; and that, therefore, it is not of the nature of the body. Whatever it is, whatsoever its attributes, its capabilities, its conditions of being, or its ultimate destiny, the dissolution of the body, which liberates it from its earthly connections, leaves its vitality untouched and its intrinsic energies unimpaired. With its bodily connection severed, it enters a new soul-life, a new state, where it finds new associations and new activities, all adapted to its needs, and all adjusted to the development of its spiritual life, and looking to the final glory awaiting it in the "manifestation of the sons of God."

The criticisms of soul sleepers and destructionists are not forgotten, but we fail to find any force in them. The fact that the word here rendered "soul is," in a few instances and other connections, rendered "life," proves nothing against its proper meaning in these passages. It is the proper word for soul, and is not the proper word for life, and it is only used in the sense of "life" in view of the fact that its connection with the body depends upon the life of the body. It is this life of the body with which the soul is contrasted; and one of the absurdities of all the reasoning of materialists on this point is seen in their continuous habit of confounding these two things which the Savior so sharply distinguished and so plainly contrasted. The soul is not the life of the body, because the soul does not die, or is not destroyed when the body is killed. The life of the body is destroyed, but the soul is not.

There are many facts mentioned in the Scriptures which are rich in suggestiveness at least on this subject. The transfiguration of Christ revealed the presence of Moses, who had been dead many hundreds of years. There is no intimation that he appeared in a glorified body, or that he had yet experienced the resurrection of the dead; nor dare we imagine that the scene was merely phenomenal, deceiving the disciples by an optical illusion, in which phantoms played the part of historical personages. The testimony is too plain. Moses and Elias appeared talking with Jesus, and they talked about the decease of Jesus at Jerusalem. To the Sadducees, who denied the separate existence of the soul, as they did the existence of angels, Christ once said concerning Abraham, Isaac, and Jacob, "they live," although they had been so long dead. There is a sense in which these old Patriarchs were alive, while their bodies slumbered in the grave. We may say of them, as the apostle said of David, "They are dead and buried." "They are not ascended into the heavens;" their resurrection is not yet accomplished; yet they "all live unto him." Their souls did not die with their bodies.

And so the parable of the rich man and Lazarus, if it be a parable, represents Lazarus as living with Abraham, after he had died in poverty at the rich man's gate; and it also represents the rich man as existing in the painful consciousness of torment, after he was dead and buried. But it is said that these are only appearances and representations, not realities. Let us be careful here. It matters nothing whether this Scripture be taken as a parable or a history, so far as its meaning is concerned; but, whatever view we take, it must be conceded that Christ *represented* these men as continuing to exist after death. Now, that representation was either true or false. Men exist after death, or they do not. Christ represented them as existing. The people to whom the representation was made believed it true, and the Savior knew that they believed it true, and that if he did not correct their impressions they would be confirmed in this belief; yet he did not attempt to controvert their prevailing thought, but made this representation of the state of the dead in good faith, and with the most impressive silence respecting any misapprehension likely to arise in the minds of any who believed in the separate existence of the soul. What if this representation is parable? Christ's parables are not fables. He did not deal in fiction. Every parable he uttered was founded in fact. This point is worthy of particular note, especially as sometimes reference is made to the parables of our Lord to justify the use of fiction, as a suitable medium through which to communicate religious truth. Whether it be right or wrong to use fiction, or whether it be possible to employ it to advantage or not, it can not be shown that Christ resorted to it. We must therefore conclude that when he represented the souls of men as in existence after death, he meant that we should believe that they do exist. He spoke of the existence of spirits "without flesh and bones," and of the continued life of patriarchs and prophets, in such a way as to confirm the Pharisees, who believed in these things, as against the Sadducees, who disbelieved them.

We are unable to see any other way of interpreting our Lord's response to the appeal of the dying penitent, "To-day shalt thou be with me in paradise," than as teaching an immediate entrance of the soul into conscious rest. After studying what the critics have said about the punctuation of this text, and about Oriental customs, and the meaning of the word "paradise," our conviction remains undisturbed. Paul was caught up into "paradise," and he spoke of it as the "third heaven," but he betrays no consciousness of the presence of his body, or of its participation in the rapture of the soul. Indeed, he could not tell but that he was "out of the body" in that wonderful experience, which shows that he did not doubt the possibility of the disembodied existence. Christ entered paradise the day he was crucified, and the soul of the penitent entered "with him," without awaiting the coming of the Son of man in the clouds of heaven.

In harmony with this view there is another fact of special significance. It is that when the Savior comes in the clouds with the angels, with the sound of the trumpet to raise the dead, the saints are to come with him. "When Christ, who is our life, shall appear, then shall ye also appear with him in glory." "For if we believe that Christ died and rose again, even so them also which sleep in Jesus will God bring with him." During the intervening period they are "absent from the body and present with the Lord," and when he comes it will be "with all his saints," as well as with the angels. It can not be that they will then appear "with him" in full possession of their resurrection bodies; for in this respect they are then to be "caught up," in company with those who are "alive and remain," "to meet the Lord in the air." They come with him, resume their rising bodies, and with the living, translated saints, are caught up to be forever with the Lord.

This brings us to a passage bearing on the subject, and requiring careful study. It extends from 2 Corinthians iv, 16, to the ninth verse of the chapter following—too long to transcribe here. Notwithstanding the division of chapters this is a single paragraph, and the key-note is struck in the opposite tendencies of the "outward man" and the "inward man." Much has been said about the peculiar language here employed, but the result of the most critical scrutiny is, that the most obvious sense of the words is the true sense. The "outward man" is the body, and the "inward man" is the soul. The body is "perishing," gradually going down to death; but the soul is not perishing. The "inward" differs from the "outward man" in nature, substance, and quality; it is not subject to the same laws of life, nor liable to the same fate in death. So opposite are these two natures, manifesting a veritable duality in each individual, that as one yields to the inevitable law of dissolution, the other becomes more and more vigorous, and shows itself possessed of additional powers yet to unfold, as it escapes the depressions and enthrallments of its connection with a nature tending to death. "For which cause we faint not; but though our outward man perish, yet the inward man is renewed day by day." Hence the apostle spoke of the afflictions of the body, even to dissolution, as being light and momentary. The soul survives them all, and enters the higher state scarcely conscious of the burden left behind, except as its participation in the afflictions of earth enhances its appreciation of the exceedingly abundant glory which is eternal. And this glory appears to the eye of faith while the burden is yet being borne, and reveals itself with greater clearness and increasing value, as the "inward man" turns away from material things, which are temporal, and fixes its gaze upon the realities of the world to come. "The things which are not seen are eternal." And this approximation of the soul to invisible things is not arrested by the dissolution of the "outward man." The whole tendency during the bodily life is in the opposite direction, and it can not be that the culmination of the temporary affliction will reverse the order of all previous experience. "For we know that if our earthly house of this tabernacle were dissolved, we have a building of God, a house not made with hands, eternal in the heavens." The "outward man" here becomes our "earthly house," distinguished from a permanent home or dwelling place, and giving the character of a "tabernacle," so that the soul's stay on earth is merely a tent-life. Its connection with this world is veiled and unseen, and is preparatory to a higher life and an enduring residence in the spiritual state. In grasping the idea of this higher life, and giving it expression as uninterrupted by death, the apostle blends metaphors, recognizing the continued life of the soul, and yet reaching out in thought to the everlasting habitations beyond the resurrection. This involves some obscurity, and calls for careful observance of the scope of the argument. We must, therefore, before becoming confused with this mingling of metaphors, note the emphatic point in the statement. It is that which indicates the time when the soul is to have the dwelling place which is not the "earthly house of this tabernacle." Whatever the "building of God" may mean in its ultimate signification, it is to receive the soul, and become the house or dwelling-place of the "inward man" during the time the "outward man," the body or "tabernacle," is lying in the dust of death. The earthly house will dissolve, and then the building of God will be occupied. It is well, also, to observe the leading points of contrast in this language. It is not the perishing body with the resurrection body, but the temporary residence of the soul on earth with its permanent abode in heaven. This puts the whole future existence in opposition to the brief life in this world, making the contrast more striking and impressive than a mere antithetic comparison of the natural and the spiritual body. And the fact that the final glory of the redeemed is brought into the account, does not necessarily imply that its fullest development will be found in the first experiences of the soul after leaving the body; for the idea of a progressive development is by no means incompatible with Scriptural thoughts and figures, and is not excluded by the metaphors here introduced.

The great fact postulated with emphasis is, that in passing out of the dying body, the conscious selfhood, the "inward man," enters upon a career of everlasting enjoyment, which beginning, as it does, in a disembodied state, continues its approach to the infinite source of blessedness, until the redemption of the body itself is accomplished. The groaning in this tabernacle is easily understood, but the use of the words "clothed" and "unclothed" induces a slight obscurity. The building of God, the house not made with hands, appears to become at once the dwelling place and the clothing of the soul. It supplies the place of the body, and of the dwelling place of the body. In the truest sense it becomes the "home of the soul"— "the house from heaven," or of heavenly nature and origin. The language, confessedly obscure, may, without violence, imply an investiture of the soul with some spiritual form and vehicle, which shall ultimately take upon itself the resurrection body, and make the connecting link between the undying nature and that which out of corruption shall put on immortality. The life on earth is a mystery, and the life in heaven is not less mysterious. But there is no obscurity in this language that needs hinder us in gathering the force of the argument. The fact is plain that the "inward man," which does not perish with the "outward man," enters at once the building of God; it rises from earth to heaven, and begins its eternal life; but this is not all that was in the apostle's thought. He saw in that house not made with hands all needful provision for the permanent home, and while groaning in this earthly tabernacle, and contemplating the coming blessedness, he longed first to be disembodied and then to be finally established in the home of the redeemed, where "mortality is swallowed up of life"—an expression which looks to the ultimate deliverance of the body from the dominion of death.

After this allusion to the ultimate triumph, the apostle comes back to the leading thought of immediate union with Christ, when death occurs. "Therefore," in view of all the provisions for the soul, when done with earth, "we are always confident, knowing that whilst we are at home in the body we are absent from the Lord (for we walk by faith, not by sight); we are confident, I say, and willing rather to be absent from the body, and to be present with the Lord." In the thought of the apostle there is a conscious selfhood which is distinguishable from the body, which now lives in the body, but neither blends with it nor depends upon it so as to be incapable of another life, and which is not destined to share all the experiences of the physical nature. This interior selfhood grows stronger while the body grows weaker; it departs from the body in death, but does not die; and when the body falls into dust, it returns to God who gave it. It is then "absent from the body," yet still living, being "present with the Lord." It was in view of this continued life of the proper person, that our Savior said, "If any man keep my saying he shall never see death." The separate life of the soul is thus plainly revealed, and appears so positively interwoven with these Scriptures that we can not explain them with consistency or satisfaction without taking this doctrine as an established truth. And to be "present with the Lord" means more than

SEPARATE EXISTENCE OF THE SOUL.

to lose connection with earth. Paul saw in it something desirable, something far better than to live in the body, and spoke as if anxious for the consummation: "For I am in a strait betwixt two, having a desire to depart and to be with Christ, which is far better." This can mean nothing less than conscious communion with Christ. Whether the selfhood that departs from the body finds prepared for it a special vehicle in which to live, or whether the soul itself forms a spiritual vestment for the conscious self and divine life within it, or whether the soul, including all the qualities and characteristics of the spiritual nature remains "unclothed" till the period of the resurrection of the dead, we may not positively affirm; but that the departed saint lives with Christ, where Christ is, and in joyful fellowship with him, is the plain sense of this passage, and agrees with the whole tenor of the apostolic writings. "Wherefore we labor, that whether present or absent, we may be accepted of him."

The scene which John describes in the Revelation, wherein appeared the company of the redeemed from earth, consisting of the one hundred and forty-four thousand of the tribes of Israel, and the innumerable multitude from all nations, clad in white robes and palms in their hands, is sufficient of itself to settle the question in hand, and can not be explained in harmony with any hypothesis that denies the soul an existence separate from the body. This scene is located in heaven, in the presence of the throne of God and of the angels, where the multitude clothed in white robes lead the devotions, while the angels respond; but they were not yet in the resurrection state. There were no crowns upon their heads. These will be bestowed in the day of Christ's coming to raise the dead, after the opening of the seventh seal; but this appearance was before the last seal was opened. In another vision John saw "the souls of them that were beheaded for the testimony of Jesus," and described them as under the altar, waiting in hope of a grand consummation yet in the future, which points to the resurrection of the dead and the retribution that follows. In both visions the happiness of the saints in the separate state is declared.

The next chapter will consider the question of suffering in the separate state—*in Hades*—and the interpretation which Universalists and other "liberalists" put upon the parable of the rich man and Lazarus, which, as we have seen, discloses the condition of the departed, and reveals conscious being and actual suffering after death.

Chapter VI.

SUFFERING IN HADES.

HADES is the separate state of souls. It is the unseen world. Men die in all conditions. Some die in their sins. Do they suffer after death? We propose to answer this question by studying and applying that remarkable passage of Scripture in Luke xvi, 19–31, which is sometimes called the parable of the rich man and Lazarus, and which, for our present purpose, we shall regard as a parable.

The question sometimes raised as to whether this is parable or history is unimportant, for the reason that all our Savior's parables are founded on fact or are true to fact. This distinguishes them from fables, and gives their lessons a certainty and force that fables could not give. It is fact that sowers go forth to sow; that tares grow with the wheat; that fishermen gather the good and bad into their nets; that the mustard-seed grows to be a large herb; that leaven leavens the meal; and it is fact that both rich and poor men die—that both the righteous and the wicked enter the unseen state. Then, whether it be true or false that a particular rich man died, and was buried, and lifted up his eyes in *Hades*, in torment, one thing is certain—Christ represented this state of things. Did he represent a state of things as true which is not true? Did he adopt a falsehood and make it into a parable? This is incredible; and yet if the representation of the rich man in *Hades*, in torment after death, does not set forth what actually occurs, it must follow that the chief feature of this parable is a false representation of the state of things after death.

We agree to call this Scripture a parable; but it is neither fable nor falsehood. It represents truth. And, taken in its most obvious sense, it represents, and, therefore, teaches, that there is suffering in *Hades*. This is the great fact in the present argument.

But we wish to see what Universalists

have to say in regard to this parable. Admitting, as they mostly do, that the wicked suffer after death, there is no necessity for their denying the interpretation given above; but they do deny it, and courageously assert a different one. They do not always agree in their expositions, but in the interpretation of this parable there is such general concurrence that we safely treat it as the Universalist interpretation. In presenting it I select the words of Rev. J. M. Austin, in his debate with Dr. Holmes—page 627—for the reason that he is good authority with his class, and he presents the matter in the clearest and most concise manner possible. His language is, "What is to be understood by this parable? Let me answer briefly: 1. By the rich man, the Savior represents the Jews, especially the priests. 2. By the beggar, he represents the Gentile world. 3. By the death of the two personages, he describes the change in the circumstances of both the Jews and Gentiles, which took place at the introduction of the Gospel dispensation. 4. The rich man in Hell (*Hades*) represents the wretched condition of the Jews when God had placed them aside as his chosen people. 5. The beggar in Abraham's bosom indicates the entrance of the Gentiles into the Gospel kingdom which the Redeemer established on earth. 6. The great gulf signifies the unbelief of the Jews in the Redeemer, whereby they have been kept in their unhappy state of alienation unto this day." This application might be carried farther in regard to several minor points, but time will not allow." These "minor points," if carried out, as we learn elsewhere, would teach that the "sores" on the beggar represent the moral diseases of the Gentiles; that the "dogs" are pagan philosophers, Socrates, Plato, Aristotle, *et al;* that "licking the sores" represents the efforts of these philosophers to cure the moral maladies of the people; that the "angels" are Gospel ministers; that carrying Lazarus into Abraham's bosom, means the ministers conducting Gentiles into the fellowship of Abraham's faith; and that the "five brethren" represent—well, sometimes the body of the Jewish people, sometimes the Jews scattered beyond Judea, or whatever will best suit the occasion.

Now passing these "minor points," the extent to which this interpretation has been accepted, the influence it exerts, and the fact that so little is usually done in the way of exposing these false interpretations of important passages, will justify us in taking time to look at these six items consecutively, and testing their value.

1. Is it true that "by the rich man the Savior represents the Jews, especially the priests?" If so, all that is said of the rich man must be true of the Jews. It might be said of some of them that they fared sumptuously, for they were rich; but this can not be taken as descriptive of the Jews any more than of the nations around them. Nor can this, with the allusion to their dress, be applied to the priests as distinguished from the people; for the priests had no ecclesiastical or political life, apart from the people, that would warrant such language concerning them. They did not constitue the nation. With them the "purple and fine linen" were not the only distinguishing articles of official dress. Gold, blue, scarlet, and precious stones were equally important and con-

spicuous. And if we admit that the allusion was to the dress of the priests, we are still at a loss to know what the clothing represents in the parable. If it represents spiritual privileges, what does the sumptuous feasting represent? If worldly prosperity, when was it enjoyed? If national greatness, when were the Jews so great that neighboring nations, the Romans for instance, were "beggars" in comparison with them. The Jews, as a nation, acknowledged Abraham as their "father," but this rich man had another "father," for he said, in the parable, addressing Abraham, "I pray thee, father, that thou wouldst send him to *my father's* house." Who besides Abraham did the Jews call "father?" The rich man, after death, appealed to Abraham for help by the ministry of the beggar; but when, and in what sense, did the Jews appeal to Abraham to send Lazarus to their relief, after the change in circumstances supposed to be denoted by the death of these personages? The rich man had "five brethren," and if he represents a nation so ought they to represent nations; but what five nations could they represent?

These brethren had Moses and the prophets, that is, the Old Testament Scriptures; but what five nations, besides the Jews, had the Sacred Writings?

Many attempts have been made to tell what or whom these "five brethren" represent in the parable. Some say they represent the Jews scattered abroad, who carried the writings of Moses and the prophets with them. But the Jews scattered abroad were not separate nations. They were Jews still, and had no political or ecclesiastical existence apart from the Jews in Palestine; nor was there any thing in their condition or circumstances requiring the number "five" to designate them. And what is fatal to this hypothesis is the fact that the "five brethren" were yet at home, in their "father's house," after the rich man was in "torment." This does not answer to the condition of the dispersed Jews, scattered among the nations. And, further, the "torment" of the rich man is supposed to consist largely of the dispersion of the Jews; and if so, the "brethren" were in it first. And then the rich man desired his brethern to repent, "lest they also come into this place of torment." But when did the Jews, or even the priests, desire that the scattered Jews might repent, in order that they might escape dispersion?

But we are sometimes told that the rich man represents the priesthood, and the "five brethren" the body of the Jewish people. This is not less absurd than what we have just considered. If the rich man represented a priesthood, the brethren should do the same; but there were no other five priesthoods. Besides this, the priesthood of the Jews had no national or political existence apart from the body of the people, and consequently it could not die a political death to be represented by the death of the rich man in the parable. And, further, the rich man was dead, buried, and in torment before his brethren were dead; for they were yet alive, and in his father's house, and supposed to be in reach of repentance, when he implored Abraham to send Lazarus to them. But the Jewish priesthood was not ecclesiastically or politically dead, before the body of the Jewish people experienced a like calamity. Nor did the Jewish priests, so far as is known, ever express any desire that the body of the people should repent, especially of the sin of rejecting the Messiah which brought their woe upon them—much less that Lazarus, the Gentile world, should be sent to induce them to repent—lest they also should come into the same unhappy condition with themselves. But this is enough to show the absurdity of the statement that "by the rich man the Savior represented the Jews, especially the priests."

"2. By the beggar he represents the Gentile world." Is this true? If so all that is said in the parable about Lazarus, must in some way apply to the Gentile world. The spiritual poverty and helplessness of the Gentiles might be fitly enough represented by a beggar, clothed in rags and covered with sores; but, then, the relation to the rich man, in which the beggar is placed in the parable, fails utterly to represent the relation of the Gentiles to the Jews. The Gentiles never besought the Jews to relieve their spiritual necessities. The begging of Lazarus at the rich man's gate finds no parallel in the history of the nations, and certainly not in the relation of the Gentiles to the Jews. The Gentiles were not aware of their spiritual poverty, and if they had been oppressed with the consciousness of their destitution, they would not have gone to the Jews or the Jewish priests for relief. There is no sense in which they desired to be fed with the crumbs which fell from the Jewish table.

It is claimed that the death of the rich man represents the political death of the Jews. Mr. Austin expresses himself cautiously, calling it a "change of circumstances;" but this is what is meant, as we learn from his other writings as well as from other authors of the same school. But if so, the death of Lazarus must represent a political death likewise. Then, whose political death could it represent? The Gentile world died no political death. The death of Lazarus bettered his condition; but political death to the nations is not usually looked upon as a blessing. New political life may be gained after a political death which will be better than the old, but this is not the necessary nor the ordinary result. We seek in vain through all the history of the nations for any event to correspond with the subversion of the Jewish polity, or to be called a political death on the part of the Gentiles. But the rich man and Lazarus both died, the one as certainly as the other, and it will not do to assume that one represented a political death, and the other some other kind of death. This is not allowable, and if it were, the other kind of death, in the Gentile world, is not discoverable. It was not a moral death, for the Gentiles were morally dead before, and moral death does not improve the condition of individuals or nations. It was not a "death unto sin," for the Gentiles did not die unto sin. Individuals among Jews and Gentiles "died unto sin," as they believed on Christ, but this personal experience does not answer to the death of the beggar in any intelligible sense. The event of death is not a suitable figure with which to represent a change of circumstances in individuals or nations, which is to result in the bettering of the condition of the subject of it, unless the nature of the change is so distinctly marked as to preclude the possibility of mistake in regard to it.

The rich man's prayer, in this parable,

disproves the assumption that the beggar represented the Gentile world. "Send Lazarus that he may dip the tip of his finger in water, and cool my tongue." Did Christ represent him as requesting that the Gentile world might be sent to his relief? Did the Jews ever pray for the mitigation of their sufferings through the ministration of the Gentiles? "Send him to my father's house, for I have five brethren, that he may testify unto them," Who can believe that the Jewish nation, or priesthood, is here represented as asking Abraham to send the Gentiles to relieve its own suffering, and to warn its brethren? But it may be said that this figurative language denotes the anxiety of the Jews, after their dispersion, to obtain the doctrines of the Gospel, then in possession of the Gentiles. Then why was the prayer addressed to Abraham? and why has this anxiety of the Jews to receive the Gospel at the hands of the Gentiles never been discovered? And since those who have the Gospel are always ready to impart it to others, why was this request denied? The truth is the Jews have never sought to mitigate their sufferings by the consolations of the Gospel since their dispersion, any more than the Gentiles previously desired to be fed on the crumbs of Judaism. This explanation of the chief characters of this parable is, therefore, a failure. It is without foundation in fact, reason, or analogy, and is unsupported by any authority, and must be abandoned as a vain invention, devised for the support of a distressed theory.

"3. By the death of the two personages, he describes the change in the circumstances of both the Jews and Gentiles, which took place at the introduction of the Gospel dispensation." This is indefinite, not to say ambiguous. Nevertheless we can learn its import with a little effort. This author is also the author of the "Universalist Catechism on the Parables;" and from the catechism, and from the writings of others of the same faith, we find that the meaning is, that the Jewish nation died politically, while the Gentiles died unto sin—making the death of the rich man signify a national event, and that of the beggar represent what is purely a matter of individual experience! But where is the authority for interpreting these deaths in this way? We ask in vain. The interpretation is arbitrary, forced, unnatural, inharmonious, impossible. If one death was a national event, so was the other; and if one was a death unto sin, so was the other. Both died the same kind of death, however changed their circumstances after death. But both could not have been national political deaths, for there was no political death in the Gentile world to be represented by the death of Lazarus. Nor could both have been a death unto sin; for the Jews did not die unto sin. Besides, Lazarus died first, and if his death signified the conversion of the Gentiles, they should have been converted before the Jews died politically; but they were not. Both died suddenly; but the change in the circumstances of the Jews and Gentiles did not take place suddenly, but after long preparation, and after a long struggle, and after having been the subject of prophecy for many years. The facts are all against this interpretation.

The angels carried Lazarus into Abraham's bosom. This means something. Mr. Austin says, "This is an allusion to the angels, messengers, or preachers of the Gospel, by whom the Gentiles were brought into the belief of the same promises and faith in Christ with which Abraham was blessed." (Catechism, p. 128.) But we have no evidence that the phrase "Abraham's bosom" was ever understood among the Jews as signifying Church privileges or faith in Christ. On the contrary, the Jews used it for a different purpose, and always with reference to the happiness of the souls of the righteous after death. Hence the Babylonish Talmud, "Holy men did all they could to detain Rabbi Judah here, but angels carried him to heaven; now he sits in Abraham's bosom."

The Jews also believed in the existence of angels; that is, the great mass of the Jewish people did, for the skepticism of the Sadducees affected the popular mind but slightly; and hence, without notice of a different use of the word, they would understand this term as relating to heavenly intelligences, in whose existence and ministrations they had unquestioning faith. The disciples themselves were not angels, nor did they become angels when they became apostles. In a few instances this word is applied, figuratively, to the ministers in the Church, but so as not to mislead or become a personal appellation. It was impossible, when this parable was spoken, that the disciples should apply this part of it to themselves; and it is certain that the first Christians never interpreted these words in any such sense as that we are considering. If the angels carrying Lazarus into Abraham's bosom after death represented Gospel ministers conducting Gentiles into the faith of Abraham, is it not strange that the rich man saw him in that place of comfort so soon after his own death, when such large portions of the Gentiles remain to this day destitute of the knowledge of Christ and the faith of Abraham?

Again, it appears that one going from Abraham, where Lazarus was, to the rich man's father's house, was such an event as could be described as one rising from the dead. But if the Church should send missionaries to preach the Gospel to the Jews, or to any people represented by the "five brethren," the appearance of such missionaries could not be called a resurrection from the dead, without the severest strain upon the language, and inexcusable obscurity. And at this point our author overleaps himself, and yields the whole ground, though inadvertently, by illustrating this language by the rising again of the other Lazarus and by the resurrection of Christ himself, both of which were literal resurrections. If one going from the state Lazarus was in, to the "five brethren," was a rising from the dead, illustrated by the resurrection of Christ or by the calling of the other Lazarus out of his grave, it is simply absurd to think of the death of Lazarus as any thing other than a literal death. But if this rising from the dead, in the parable, be not fitly illustrated by these literal examples, we still inquire as to its meaning, and receive no answer. Upon this point our "liberal" expositors are as silent as the grave.

"4. The rich man in Hell (*Hades*) represents the wretched condition of the Jews, when God had placed them aside as his chosen people." As the meaning of the word *Hades* is not the point in question just now, we shall not dwell on that, but try to weigh the proposition that applies the term, figuratively, to the "wretched condition of the Jews" in this world. If there were nothing like wretchedness in the literal *Hades*, it could not be used very well as a figure of wretchedness here. If there were no degradation there,— if all were silent unconsciousness, as some hold, or if all were peace and happiness, as others claim,— it would not, as a metaphor or simile, present a very dark picture of degradation and wretchedness, to represent the results of sin in this life.

Mr. Austin elsewhere says, "that in representing the rich man as being tormented in *Hades*, Jesus but repeated the popular notions of that age in regard to the condition of the wicked in the invisible world." (Catechism p. 135.) This is a concession of tremendous import, but it was not an inadvertence. It is a fact which an intelligent Universalist would not attempt to deny. Upon this same point, the Rev. I. D. Williamson, D. D,— than whom there is no better Universalist authority, — uses the following language: "Around him [Christ] were the mammon-worshiping Pharisees, glorying in their wealth and despising the poor, clinging to the law, and rejecting the Gospel, notwithstanding they saw it attested with signs and miracles before their eyes. They believed that in *Hades*, or 'Hell' as it is translated in the text, there were two apartments—one for the righteous and one for the wicked—and made no doubt that they should dwell with Abraham in bliss, while the poor and the despised, the publicans and the sinners, would be cast out and made to dwell in torments. Our Savior fitted his discourse to his hearers; he founded his parable precisely upon their views, and in the end taught them that, by their own showing, instead of being above others, they were worse than those they despised." (Lectures, p. 182.)

There can be no doubt that the Jews believed in "torment," in Hades, after death. The intelligent of all classes, and of all grades of "liberalistic" thought, agree to this. But could our Savior, in the presence of this general sentiment, "repeat the popular notions of that age," and "found his parable precisely" upon the views of the people addressed, without impressing them that he approved the "popular notion" in regard to the condition of the wicked in the invisible world? Would he "repeat the popular notions of the age," and found a parable upon them, and leave them uncontradicted, if his purpose was to disapprove those notions, and to teach a different doctrine by applying the language to something in this world which they were accustomed to apply only to the state of the dead? The supposition that he would is preposterous. The very fact, so fully admitted, that he repeated the popular notions of the people, proves unanswerably that he did not speak of torment in *Hades* after death for the purpose of representing the "wretched condition of the Jews" in this world. Neither the Jews in general, nor his own disciples, could have understood him if he intended any such thing. If he intended to be understood, he must have regarded the popular opinions of the Jews as sufficiently correct to receive this mark of approval. As an honest man, he could not allude to the popular notions prevailing all around him, and use them uncontradicted, for any purpose whatever, if they were erroneous. If the popular notion on this subject was wrong, his business was to correct it, which he never did.

"5. The beggar in Abraham's bosom indicates the entrance of the Gentiles into the Gospel kingdom, which the Redeemer established on earth." But the Gentiles have not all entered the Gospel kingdom. Multitudes of them remain in the darkness of heathenism. Their conversion is not accomplished suddenly and easily, like the angels carrying a soul to paradise, but slowly, and with much labor and patient waiting, they are to be brought under the influence of the Gospel of Christ. And the Gospel kingdom has never been called "Abraham's bosom." This phrase was familiar to the Jews, and bore a different meaning, as we have seen. This new application of it is without precedent or authority, and is contrary to established usage. Moreover, if the "angels" are Gospel ministers, as is claimed, they have as much right to carry the Jews as the Gentiles into the Gospel kingdom. They are ready to perform this gracious office for any and all classes alike. They were commissioned to "preach the Gospel to every creature," and were directed to open their ministry at home among the Jews, "beginning at Jerusalem." The Gospel is the power of God unto salvation to every one that believeth, "to the Jew first, and also to the Greek." And, finally on this point, the rich man acknowledged that Lazarus was in "Abraham's bosom," and sought relief at his hands; but the Jews have never acknowledged the Gentiles to be in possession of the true faith and blessing of Abraham, nor sought spiritual comfort at the hands of Gentile Christians.

"6. The great gulf signifies the unbelief of the Jews in the Redeemer, whereby they have been kept in their unhappy state of alienation unto this day." This is unfounded assertion. The gulf was "fixed" between the parties. It was appointed and established by divine ordination. The unbelief of the Jews was sufficiently stubborn, and in that sense "fixed," but it was not appointed nor ordained of God. It was not the product of divine power. On the contrary, they were guilty of their own unbelief. They were favored with evidences enough to convince them of the Messiahship of Jesus, but they shut their eyes to the light. They "fixed" their own unbelief, but "father Abraham" did not intimate to the rich man that he had fixed the gulf himself. It was his fault that he was on the wrong side of it, but the gulf was there without his agency.

And this "gulf" could not be crossed. The separation between the parties was final. Think of this, ye who imagine probation in *Hades!* But the unbelief of the Jews in this life was not necessarily so permanent as this gulf. However terrible their blindness and inveterate their prejudices, the removal of the unbelief of living Jews has never been rated an impossibility. The first converts to Christianity were from the Jews, and in the early age of the Church many thousands of that people embraced the Gospel; and in every period of the Church's history some portions of this wonderful people have yielded to the power of truth, and found redemption in Jesus Christ. There has always been "a remnant according to the election of grace." Every instance of the conversion of a Jew is a contradiction to this interpretation of the "great gulf." And these contradictions will go on; for if the prophecies may be accepted as trustworthy, the Jews will yet, as a race, give up their unbelief, embrace the Gospel, and share the blessings of the Redeemer's kingdom. The middle wall between the Jews and Gentiles has been broken down. All distinctions on account of nationality have been destroyed, so that sinners of all nations stand on the same ground with respect to the provisions of the Gospel and the terms of salvation. "For there is no difference between Jew and Greek; for the same Lord over all is rich unto all that call upon him."

It is, therefore, evident that God's rejection of the Jews from his covenant through unbelief, by which they were set aside from being his peculiar people "fixed" no impassable gulf between them and the Church of Christ on earth. They were broken off from the good olive-tree by their unbelief, but God is able to graft them in again, and when the blindness which happened to them shall pass away, their conversion will prove to be the crowning achievement of the Gospel on earth.

This "gulf" is so important a feature of this parable that we ought to be sure of our ground with respect to it, because of its bearing on the general subject in hand, independently of the interpretation we have been considering. Whatever its nature or import, the "gulf" is represented as being "fixed" between parties that were dead. Abraham, who appears in this connection, had been dead, literally, for hundreds of years; Lazarus had died and been carried by angels into Abraham's bosom; the rich man also had died and had been buried before the gulf appears. The fact that Abraham was a real person, and was literally dead, is not questioned. Nor is it denied that Lazarus is represented as being with him, and therefore dead in the same sense, and enjoying the comforts of the same spiritual state that Abraham was enjoying. No one can question that the *representation* is of the state of the dead. Abraham, who was dead, was on one side of the "gulf" with Lazarus, who had died, in his bosom, or in intimate fellowship with him; and the rich man, who had also died and been buried, was on the other side of it. The gulf was, therefore, between the dead; and if no such separation between the dead actually exists in the invisible world, the representation is misleading, and the parable is based on falsehood! No matter what application be made of the parable to things in this world, or how the "gulf" be metaphorically used with reference to unbelief or any thing else, if the state of the dead be not as represented, the whole thing is worse than fiction and utterly meaningless.

To allege that this representation of the state of the dead is fiction, is to rob it of the dignity of a parable and reduce it to the grade of an ill-contrived riddle. The parables of our Lord were not enigmatical representations of things that existed only in the fancy, calculated to bewilder and confound his hearers, but they were pointed narrations of fact, designed to illustrate truth, and to impress the understanding and the conscience. They were adapted to his hearers, the Jews, who knew nothing of the far-fetched ideas the modern "liberalists" seek to fasten on this one, and who could not possibly have understood any thing of his meaning, neither they nor his own disciples, if the modern interpretation is correct, nor did any one succeed in guessing it for the period of eighteen hundred years. And in this parable, which is not fiction, Christ represented a state of suffering or "torment" in *Hades*. This no man calls in question, who believes or interprets the Holy Scriptures. And upon this idea of suffering in *Hades*, which his hearers believed to be the truth, he founded his parable. So say the most distinguished opposers of the doctrine of eternal punishment, as well as the learned of all classes. Then how is it possible to avoid the conclusion that he meant to sanction the doctrine of punishment in *Hades?*

The Jews believed in future and eternal punishment to the wicked, and nothing short of a positive declaration to the contrary would prevent them from understanding this parable as confirming their faith. They believed that the righteous, at death, were taken to a place of rest, which they called Abraham's bosom; and that the wicked, at death, entered *Hades*, where they were "tormented" till the judgment. Addressing men who believed all this, the Savior delivered this parable for the purpose of reproving the sin of covetousness. He taught them herein that wealth would not secure the favor of God; that worldly prosperity was no mark of the divine approval; but that the richest of them might perish and suffer all the torment of the lost in the invisible world in spite of their abundance. The illustration was striking, easily comprehended, and easily applied, and the lesson worthy the teacher and the occasion. Having just taught them by another parable that they could not serve God and mammon; that their possessions were not their own; that they were only stewards of the good things of this life, and must give account of their stewardship, he now carried their minds to the future, to see the outcome of a life of sinful indulgence, as contrasted with that of a virtuous life of poverty and suffering. The rich man was described as luxuriating in all the world could give, and the poor man as reaching the lowest point of humiliation and want. Then both die, and the scene is changed. The rich man from his palace sank down to torment, and the beggar left his rags and ascended to honor and bliss. Then how vain are riches! How foolish and wicked the sin of covetousness!

Just here our "liberal" friends resort to ridicule, making themselves merry over what they call the absurdities of our "literal interpretations." They play on the words "bosom," "eyes," "tongue," "gulf," "flames," representing that we are obliged to take every word in its literal sense, if we apply the parable to the state of the dead literally. In this they misapprehend the facts, and spend their strength on false issues. The language is figurative, and we treat it accordingly, only insisting that correct rules of interpretation be applied to it. Of necessity words relating to material things must be used metaphorically when applied to the spiritual state. The fact of suffering after death in *Hades* is clearly taught, though its nature is not explained. The "bosom," the "eyes," and the "tongue" are metaphors, undoubtedly; but the "comfort" is real, on the one hand, and the "torment," on the other. We may infer that the suffering is not corporeal, in the absence of the body, but we need not attempt to comprehend it or try to measure its intensity. Spiritual though it be, it is represented as torment, and the word "flames" misleads no one. No doubt it involves the consciousness of forfeited good, and that self-reproach and remorse are elements in the cup of woe.

And here we meet such questions as the following, supposed to indicate difficulties: "Is hell so near to heaven as this? Must the saints in heaven forever hear the wails and groans, the cursings and blasphemings, of the lost? Must they witness the agonies and listen to the filthy mutterings of the condemned forever and ever?" But this is not the final Hell. It is *Hades*, not *Gehenna*. And this reported conversation need not imply that the spirits of the departed literally talk across the gulf. It reveals the sentiments and feelings of the parties, and the experiences of disembodied souls can only be declared to us in language understood on earth; so that it is perfectly natural that they should be described as clothing their thoughts in words. But this much is apparent. The representation shows that rich, ungodly men, will find themselves in such condition after death, that they would gladly exchange places with the poorest of earth safely landed in heaven. This is the material import of this reported conversation, which, though figuratively expressed, has a definite signification. It opens the very chambers of the souls of the departed, and discloses their interior emotions and most secret thoughts, and that without absurdity and without mistake.

And here we leave the subject. The interpretation of the "liberalists" is unauthorized and absurd, while the view we take yields a meaning in perfect harmony with the scope and design of the parable, and with the condition of those who heard it.

Chapter VII.

FIXEDNESS OF CHARACTER IN HADES.

CHARACTER is what a man is, not what he seems. It is the real man, embracing his principles, his passions and dispositions, and particularly his power to select motives and act upon his convictions. It is not the aggregation of the forces and influences that surround and make up the daily life, but the inward man, as surrounded and affected, as modified and impressed, by these outward influences, and as he comes to be in the exercise of his own powers.

Character is largely an acquisition. Men are, in character, what they become in contact with the educational and social influences under which they grow up, and the business pursuits that occupy their time and employ their energies. True, there is a substratum of character in each, a bent of mind, or certain texture of spirit, that receives or repels the impressions that come from without; and this intrinsic nature, with its idiosyncrasies of temper and will, is the real selfhood of the person, the foundation, so to speak, on which character is builded; and in this selfhood is found the basis of responsibility, because here, in the essential nature, is found the rationality and volitional power essential to responsibility. We can not therefore admit that character is the creature of circumstances or of education; for beneath all the extrinsic forces contributing to the formation of character, this invincible selfhood retains the power of choice, and the self-determining right that gives the final bent and impulse to the soul. Nevertheless those outward things do greatly affect the character. They control largely our views of life. They color the moral atmosphere in which we dwell. In the midst of their clamor and rush for ascendency the selfhood too often lies dormant, or passively yields to the dominant force, and receives impressions and biases without active choice. In such cases responsibility is not superseded, although the power that supports it is not exercised.

There is in us a tendency towards fixedness of character. In early life we are fickle, fond of changes, and susceptible of impressions that easily move us in one direction or another, according to whim or fancy. But as years advance, and we come in contact with the world, and realize the sternness of the battle of life, novelty loses its charms, new sensations are less controlling, new emotions arise less readily, and new impulses less easily turn us out of our accustomed ways. The power of choice, having learned to run in one direction, whether by passive submission or active exertion, naturally adheres to its course, and proportionately loses the facility if not the ability to accept different motives.

And yet, while we are in this world, there is a possibility of change in dispositions, in affections, in habits, in character. But the time comes when this is a bare possibility, the probability being strongly against it. The instances of moral changes in advanced life are rare, and the influences producing them almost always extraordinary; yet they sometimes do occur. The hoary sinner may be converted; for the power of Divine grace is not entirely subject to the rules and conditions of ordinary influences. It will sometimes overleap the bounds of ordinary experience and accomplish wonders. Then, under its quickening energies, habit, powerful and long continued, may be overcome. They that are accustomed to do evil may learn to do good. And yet the Ethiopian does not change his skin nor the leopard his spots. Those long habituated to sin, do not of their own energies leap out of its meshes, break the chains that bound them, and secure deliverance from thralldom. Their deliverance is of God. They become prodigies of mercy, and illustrations of the possibility of grace, such as we have no warrant for expecting will be often repeated.

The possibility of change is inseparable from probation. So soon as a subject of moral government reaches a state of confirmed holiness, so as to be incapable of defection, it is impossible to apply the term "probation" to his state, in any intelligible sense. He is no longer on trial whose character is unalterable, whose destiny is sealed.

FIXEDNESS OF CHARACTER IN HADES.

If any sink so far into the mire of sensuality as to deaden their moral sensibilities, and thereby render repentance impossible, while yet in this world of probation, this fixedness of character closes the real trial, and the man of "reprobate mind" is already doomed. Abandoned of God and given up to his own way, with habits fixed and energies all bent to evil, he is "without God, and without hope in the world." His trial is virtually ended—his destiny is morally determined. At least he has gone beyond the ordinary limits of grace, and if saved it must be by extraordinary manifestations of the Divine Spirit, which God can give, but which we can not anticipate, and which we have no right to depend upon.

This state of moral fixedness may be reached in this world, if we read the Scriptures correctly, or if we rightly interpret the great facts of human experience which bear upon the subject. We would not say that any man absolutely passes the line of probation while yet on earth, so that all possibility of his salvation, even by the extraordinary revelations of grace, is gone; but many undoubtedly reach that degree of insensibility which renders all the ordinary appliances of the Gospel ineffectual, so that nothing but direct, supernatural agency, such as the Gospel does not promise, can bring them to repentance. But whether this desperate experience is verified in life or not, all the tendencies of human nature, and all the observable experiences we meet, are in the direction of this fixedness, so that with each day's additional indulgence in sin the cords of habit are strengthened, and the probabilities of a return to God are diminished. Sin blinds the mind and hardens the heart. Habit grows and increases its power, while it divests the person of his capability of resistance to its demands, thus in double measure intensifying its hold, and multiplying the chances that it will prove unalterable. In the light of this acknowledged tendency of habit, and of the history of the past, all regard the conversion of an aged sinner as something worthy of remark. When an active, earnest man, possessing any vigor of thought or feeling, passes the meridian of life without yielding to the Gospel, the

FIXEDNESS OF CHARACTER IN HADES. 137

common sentiment, whether embodied in expression or not, and however reluctantly owned, is, "He is joined to his idols, let him alone." This fact is stern, and even terrible to contemplate; yet it is a fact which stands out in human history with such prominence that every one is forced to see it.

This tendency to fixedness of character suggests the termination of probation and the utter impossibility of moral changes when death once removes us from this world of change. Here life is elementary. The manifest design of our earthly existence is the development of character. This world is a vast school-house, and every thing that surrounds us fills the office of teacher. We begin to learn as we begin to live, and through all our years we both give out to others and receive from others new impressions, and thus, whether we will or not, we are being educated for eternity. During this educational process change is inevitable. It is the law of our being and of our probation. But as the process advances, the changes become more and more difficult. In old age they are next to impossible. Then reason tells us they will cease forever. But reason itself can not penetrate the veil that shuts from view the mysteries of the state beyond the grave. All the indications point to death as terminating the influences and helps necessary to repentance and the regeneration of our natures. But Revelation alone can disclose the realities of the great hereafter, and speak with authority of the condition of the departed in *Hades*, and her voice should be heard in silence. And Revelation tells us that all is fixedness in the future. Not one ray of hope is held out to the thoughtless and negligent of earth, that duties undone here may there be performed, or that sins cherished here may there be repented of and forsaken. "They that go down into the pit can not hope for thy truth."

The wise man said, "There is no work, nor device, nor wisdom in the grave, whither thou goest;" and on this fact he argued the folly of postponing the duties of the present, and based his earnest appeal, "Whatsoever thy hand findeth to do, do it with thy might." It means, if it means any thing, that work neglected in life can not be done

FIXEDNESS OF CHARACTER IN HADES. 139

after death. There repentance and reformation are out of the question. Death brings the night wherein no man can work. And it is with strict application to the eternal state that Divine Revelation says, "He that is unjust let him be unjust still; he that is filthy, let him be filthy still; and he that is righteous, let him be righteous still; and he that is holy, let him be holy still." This fixedness of character which has never been found in this world as a rule, and which can not co-exist with probation and with Gospel privileges, necessarily belongs to the period after death, when it will not distinguish exceptional cases, but become the law of being, suitable to the state of retribution and destiny.

The righteous die. They enter a state of unchanging blessedness. They are confirmed in holiness. No possibility of defection throws its dark shadow across their pathway as they revel in the beatitudes of an immortal life. The period of trial is past, and the broad seal of triumph marks them as eternally saved. And the wicked die. They carry with them into the invisible world the character they formed in life. They go covered with guilt and unbelief, with understandings darkened and consciences seared; they go with the will stubborn and rebellious, and the moral nature debased, so as to contain the elements of subjective wretchedness, even if no positive penalties beyond the consciousness of loss awaited them. Where in all the Scriptures is there revealed any provision or agency intended to change their moral dispositions and bring them to repentance? Where is there even a hint that probation is continued or that a new trial is instituted? Once the veil is drawn aside, and a soul in torment after death is shown to us in search of this provision, anxious for the mitigation of his suffering; and if there could be any hope for relief, that occasion for its intimation could not have passed. But the divine teacher made no promise. The "gulf" that separated the rich man from happiness could not be crossed; and as firmly "fixed" as was that gulf is the character of every one that passes into the unseen state. There is no fact, principle, or intimation given in the Scriptures from which the moral change of the soul in death or after death can be inferred. Death stereotypes character. The purgatorial probation of Romanism is a myth. Prayers for the dead are a cheat. The soul retains its essential attributes—consciousness, memory, and will; otherwise identity is lost. These imply the power to recall the past; and the memory of a life of sin, with reflections upon mercy despised and grace rejected, will bring regret and remorse; but these moral sensations have in themselves no transforming power. They are not repentance. They are the elements of misery, and when burdened with conscious hopelessness, they oppress the soul with darkness deep and terrible enough, without the added tortures of material fire. As certainly as the soul survives the body, these moral sensations will cleave to it as a vesture, and anguish and self-reproach will follow the wicked through all the depths of the world of darkness.

The idea that God will change the character of those who die in sin, by special interposition after death, is unsupported by any passage of Scripture, and is liable to insuperable objections. We note the following: 1. It is contrary to all the passages that represent the present as the time of salvation: "Behold now is the accepted time; behold now is the day of salvation." 2. It destroys all motives to repentance drawn from the shortness of time and the uncertainty of life. 3. It encourages the wicked to neglect preparation for the future till death. 4. It breaks the force of Scriptural appeals to prepare to meet God, particularly those that are based on considerations of the future state. 5. It implies a change in the divine administration which would involve a change in God himself. Let us pursue this last thought a moment. If the wicked are changed after death, it is with their consent or without it. If with their consent, means must be employed to gain their consent which are not now employed; for all the means now employed fail, and may fail forever. If more effectual means are employed then than now, a change in the divine government is implied: for the Scriptures assure us that all the means consistent with the divine government are now employed for this purpose, and without success; and if God does all he can do to gain the sinner's consent to be saved, and then after death does more than he could do here, so as to render failure impossible, a change in his government is manifest to all who think upon it, unless it is the order of his government to give men a better chance for repentance after death than before it. But this last supposition is contrary to all the representations of this life as the day of grace and of merciful visitation. It can not, therefore, be the order of his government to afford more grace after death than in this life. But if he changes the hearts of sinners after death without their consent, the change in his government is still more marked; for it is plain not only that this is something which he does not do now, but which he can not do in harmony with the principles of his government. We know that he does not change men's hearts without their consent, and to suppose that he can, and will not, is to suppose that he prefers sin to holiness, so far as this life is concerned, in every instance in which he permits men to persist in sin. Although we know so little of the limitations of the divine nature, there is no rashness in the assumption that God prefers holiness all the time, and seeks its promotion in conformity to the law of his being and the nature of human souls.

But suppose that sinners are purified after death, without their consent, could they enjoy holiness? Could they unite with the saints in the worship and adoration of that Being against whom they had rebelled, and whom they would not consent to serve, till his resistless power destroyed their moral freedom and changed their hearts contrary to their desire? Is not forced holiness a contradiction in terms? In other words, is not freedom essential to both holiness and happiness? And if a sinner is changed into a saint without his consent, is not his freedom lost? We know that it may be said that God can infuse holiness into the soul without the sinner's consent, and without destroying his freedom, because with God all things are possible. But then it is no contradiction to this Scriptural expression, and no limitation of the divine power, to say that God can not work contradictions. He can not do and not do at the same time with reference to the same thing. Nor can a man be forced and not forced, free and not free, at the same time. And is there no contradiction in this case? If not—if God can make men holy without their consent, why does he not do it now? Why have we not a few examples of persons forced into holiness? Holiness is as desirable now as it ever will be, and God reveals himself as doing all he can consistently with his nature and government to secure it—why, then, does he not at once overrule rebellion and unbelief, and rid the universe of sin with a sweep of his right arm? If holiness were the product of power we might expect this; but, instead, it is a moral achievement, requiring the concurrence of free-will, and therefore Omnipotence awaits the march of spiritual forces which move without coercion.

If men die in sin, and enter *Hades* bearing the characters formed in this life, with the incrustations of evil habit upon their moral natures, they pass, in that condition, beyond the remedial agencies of the Gospel of grace, and perish forever, or God's government must change in its fundamental principles, and so completely, too, as to imply a change in his own nature. But God can not change; his government must abide; and fixedness of character will be the order of the invisible state. "They that go down into the pit can not hope for thy truth." Penal fires do not expiate sin. "Behold, now is the accepted time; behold, now is the day of salvation."

Chapter VIII.

GEHENNA—THE ISSUE STATED.

IN considering further the New Testament idea of Hell, it will be necessary to study the use of the word *Gehenna* more fully than we have done.

This word, more nearly than any other one in the Scriptures, corresponds in meaning with the ideas commonly attached to the English word Hell, so far as the finality of punishment is concerned, and can not, by any possibility of fair criticism, be forced to give expression to the idea of a place of temporary affliction or reformatory torment. It points to the extreme punishment of the enemies of Christ, to the last abode of the lost.

None have yet been cast into *Gehenna*, and we hazard nothing in assuming that the place itself has not been created. It amounts to nothing against the argument in hand that its locality in the universe is unknown, and that ages upon ages will yet pass before "the pit be digged for the wicked." Not even the devil has yet reached this abode, as we have seen. The fallen angels are not in *Gehenna,* but in *Tartarus;* they are not yet "punished," but are reserved under chains of darkness to be punished at the day of judgment. And so it is with the wicked dead. They too are "reserved unto the day of judgment to be punished," which is also the day of "perdition of ungodly men." They are in custody, under arrest, awaiting the revelation of the judicial decision that consigns them to the final doom.

But the "chains of darkness," under which the fallen angels are held, are not material chains. We need not suppose that they impede locomotion, or bind those on whom they rest as to locality. The devil, with his mysterious host, goes "to and fro in the earth, walking up and down in it." "As a roaring lion, he walketh about, seeking whom he may devour." This is now his sphere and his occupation; but then, after the judgment, when cast into the "lake of

GEHENNA—THE ISSUE STATED. 149

fire," his access to earth will cease, and he will tempt no more. Now he is in the invisible world—*in Hades*—wherein is darkness and torment, and this prison is *Tartarus*, but it is not *Gehenna*. When the Savior used this word he looked beyond *Tartarus* and beyond *Hades;* he looked beyond the disembodied state, beyond the resurrection and the judgment, and pointed to the last calamity of the wicked. Hence *Gehenna* is different from *Tartarus* and *Hades* in this: It receives none till after the judgment, and then it never delivers them up.

The field of controversy about this word is very narrow. In relation to its origin, history, and meaning there is scarcely any dispute. It is agreed on all hands that it is made up of two Hebrew words which literally signify the valley of Hinnon. This was the name of the valley south of Jerusalem in which the worship of Moloch had long been practiced under the idolatrous kings of Israel, and there is nothing in all the history of idolatry more degrading than the rites here celebrated. This horrid worship consisted largely in sacrificing children by burning them to death. It is said that the brazen image, which represented the monster deity, was heated with fire, and the child laid in its arms till literally roasted. While this savage cruelty was going on, in order to prevent the cries of the child being heard distinctly, so as to excite feelings of humanity, a terrific noise was kept up by the beating of drums, from which circumstance the place was called Tophet, the place of drums. At length, when the Jews were brought back to the worship of the true God, King Josiah defiled the place, that "no man should make his son or his daughter pass through the fire unto Moloch." (2 King. xxiii, 10.) From that time this place was held in the greatest abhorrence by the Jews. They devoted it to the basest purposes, by casting into it the carcasses of dead beasts, and making it the receptacle of the filth and offal of the city; and so loathsome did it become that it was found necessary to keep fires constantly burning in it in order to prevent the accumulation of putrid odor, and to guard against the generation and spread of pestilence. Criminals of the worst type were executed here, and to be burned in this valley was looked upon as the most horrible punishment any one could suffer. As time rolled on every thing conspired to render the place repulsive to the Jews, and they were not slow in carrying their conceptions of its horrors and abominations into the future world, where they were taught to expect the consummation of all wickedness and all suffering. The history of the terrible idolatry which had here been practiced; the curse pronounced upon it by the authority of kings and prophets; the filth, the putrefaction, the corruption of the atmosphere, together with the lurid fires burning by day and night, all combined to make it appalling beyond description. In the days of Christ it had long been regarded as a lively emblem of the punishment of the enemies of God, and he but conformed to the custom of the Jews in using it as a symbol of the perdition awaiting the wicked in the future state.

Thus far we go hand in hand with nearly all whose company is desirable. For scholars, critics, and commentators, of all creeds and all classes, substantially agree in this representation of *Gehenna;* and it is generally agreed that in the discourses of our Lord, this literal valley of Hinnom is the emblem of the punishment which he declared to be the portion of unbelievers. Where, then, is the issue? It does not relate to the origin, history, or meaning of the word in question, or scarcely to its use, but almost solely to the application of it as a symbol. The fact that it symbolized punishment is not in question, but the point to be determined is whether it symbolized temporal or eternal punishment. Here we find divergence. Some hold that all the punishment pictured to the mind by this forcible symbol was temporal, and that particular reference was had to the national calamities about to befall the Jews. This is the view taken by most Universalists, and concurred in by other "liberalists" who respect the authority of the Scriptures, and yet reject eternal retributions. With others, who doubt inspiration, and rest their disbelief on philosophical speculations, we have nothing to do in this inquiry. Our business is with the new Testament, and those who receive it as the word of God, accepting its

decisions as final in all questions of doctrine.
We honor the opinions of such, and propose
to treat them respectfully and fairly, while
we shall not spare either premise or conclusion which is not sound. The question is not
whether this word is correctly translated or
not; on that point there is no issue. Nor is
it whether it is to be taken literally or to be
interpreted as a symbol; on this point there
is scarcely room for an issue. Nearly all concede its symbolical use. But what is the
punishment of which it is a symbol, and to
which it points? Does it relate to the punishment of individuals or of nations? Are
all its results reached in this world, or do they
go on in the future world? And if the punishment denoted by this word extends into
the future, is it temporary and restricted, or is
it final and eternal? In the study of these
questions we can only proceed safely as
directed by the light of the infallible Word.
We dare not lean upon lexicons or upon human authorities of any kind, only so far as
they may serve as helps in bringing us into
the light that God has given. Our appeal
shall, therefore, be to the Scriptures, to Bible

use, which is the final arbiter of Scriptural terms, and the sole authority in all that relates to faith and duty and destiny.

With the issue thus stated, and the field of controversy narrowed to legitimate dimensions, we can go forward in the study of the Scriptures with some hope of safe conclusions. But since the leaders in the Scriptural argument against eternal punishment, are the advocates of universal salvation, it will be important to have the views of such in mind. We, therefore, give a brief chapter for this purpose, not forgetting, however, that one of the peculiarities of "liberalism" is, that each man speaks for himself and represents only himself.

Chapter IX.

UNIVERSALIST EXPOSITIONS.

IT will not be possible to proceed understandingly in this investigation without considering what the opposers of eternal punishment have said in regard to this word; and Universalist writers must have precedence in this connection, since they have given shape and tone to all "liberalistic" sentiments, and furnished nearly all that passes for argument on that side of the question.

I select a few authorities of this class of unquestionable respectability, and shall regard them as representing the full force of the opposition. Rev. G. S. Weaver says: "As in a literal sense none were punished in *Gehenna* but such as had run the whole length of the career of wickedness and crime, and filled the measure of iniquity to its very brim, so in an emblematic sense none were threatened with or suffered *Gehenna* punishment but those who had taken the last steps in folly and crime. In a word, it meant the last and severest punishment, the miserable end and result of wickedness, the *finale* of human folly and crime, of human indifference to divine warnings and teachings." (Bible View of Hell, page 68.) This statement is sufficiently correct, as indicating the general meaning of the term and the sense in which Christ used it in his discourses. It fully recognizes the main fact on which every thing in the discussion hinges, and justifies the position taken in this argument that it relates only to the last calamity that shall befall the wicked. The mistake of this writer is not in his definition of the word, nor in his assumption that it is to be understood in the emblematic sense, but simply in his application of the emblem to a punishment, which, though it be "the miserable end and result of wickedness—the *finale* of human folly and crime"— is, nevertheless, only a temporary evil, out of which the sinner shall pass into the blessedness of an eternal life. We take his definition of the terms and his description of the punishment indicated, and insist that *Gehenna* does mean "the last and severest punishment, the miserable end and result of wickedness, the *finale* of human folly and crime." By this statement we shall abide. There is not a passage in the New Testament that requires a different definition.

T. B. Thayer, another distinguished writer on the same side, says: "The word *Gehenna* or Hell, in the New Testament, is used as a symbol of any thing that was foul or repulsive; but especially as a figure of dreadful and oppressive judgments." (History and Origin of the Doctrine of Endless Punishment, page 109.) Here again, we say, true enough as a definition, though cautiously expressed. The ground is clearly taken that *Gehenna* is a symbol; and that our Savior used it as a symbol of punishment, even as a "figure of dreadful and oppressive judgments." The "dreadful and oppressive judgments," in the view of this writer, were all of temporary character, and on this side of the resurrection, so as not to interfere in the smallest degree with the eternal felicity of any on whom they might fall. But this is bare assumption, which it is not safe to admit without some authority. If a single instance could be adduced where our Savior used this word to denote temporary judgments, without any question or mistake, there would be some show of reason for the restriction of his language to the calamities experienced this side of the eternal state; but no such instance can be found.

The following questions and answers from the "Universalist Catechism," by J. M. Austin, will give us a clear view of the position of that school of teachers in relation to this word. The quotations are from pages 33, 34.

"*Question.* Are the words, valley of Hinnom, or *Gehenna*, or Tophet ever used in the Old Testament as signifying a place of endless suffering?

"*Answer.* They are not. No evidence to this effect can be adduced.

"*Ques.* How are these words used in the Old Testament?

"*Ans.* They are used as signifying temporal punishment and calamity.

"*Ques.* Is there any evidence or any probability that the meaning of these words had changed between the days of the Old Testament writers and the advent of the Redeemer?

"*Ans.* There is no evidence whatever of this description.

"*Ques.* What meaning, then, are we bound to suppose the Savior attached to these words when he used them?

"*Ans.* We are bound to believe he used them precisely as they were used in the Old Testament; namely, to signify temporal calamity and distress.

"*Ques.* With these explanations before us, how should we understand the words 'cast into Hell,' as used in the parable under consideration?

"*Ans.* We may understand them either literally, as signifying being cast into the valley of Hinnom, to be burned to death, or figuratively, as becoming involved in calamities and wars, in consequence of sinful gratifications."

This is a fair specimen of the treatment of this subject by the exponents of what has been termed "advanced thought" in Scriptural exegesis, and to multiply names and illustrations would not shed additional light. The points are adroitly put and their plausibility is unquestionable. But is there not sophistry in their arrangement and application? We shall see.

The argument in the Catechism assumes what should be established with proof; namely, that the word *Gehenna* is used in the Old Testament only with reference to temporal calamities. A few examples of its use in this sense would have been in place. But if they had been given they would not cover the real point in issue, unless all the Old Testament passages had been cited and shown to require this meaning. Indeed it is quite possible that a few passages in the prophets related primarily to temporal calamities and ultimately to the last punishment, "the *finale* of a life of folly and crime." But whatever the Old Testament usage, the next point in this exposition is utterly inadmissible. It is that no change took place in the meaning of this word after the times of the writers of the Old Testament, and that therefore Christ must have used it in the same sense, and attached to it precisely the same ideas that prevailed in their days. The facts do not justify this statement. Christ often gave a new meaning to Old Testament words and phrases, and was quite in the habit of taking the familiar things of every-day life, to which others attached ideas of only temporal significance, and applying them to things spiritual and eternal. Instances of this are manifold, and they will occur to every reader. But the statement is sophistical, in that it speaks of the meaning of the word, where not its meaning but its use was in question. The word meant the valley of Hinnom when used by the Old Testament writers, and its literal meaning was the same when the Divine Teacher used it in his discourses. But the question is, Had it not been so often used in the figurative sense, that at the time of Christ it was generally understood to be the emblem of punishment after death, and not the emblem of merely temporal calamities? This is a question of fact, and the preponderance of proof is against the assumption of the Catechism. If it were clear that Christ spoke of *Gehenna* only in the literal sense, and with strict reference to the meaning of the word, the point made by the Catechism would have some force in it. But this is not clear. Indeed the Catechism does not teach nor allow this view of the case. It holds that Christ used the word figuratively. The prophets used it both literally and figuratively. Then the real question is, Must this word, when used figuratively by our Lord, in his profound discourses concerning sin and punishment and eternal destinies, be limited to the identical signification belonging to it in the Old Testament? To state the question is to answer it. Christ, as an independent teacher, chose the language of the people and used figures that were familiar to all, and clothed them with his own ideas, often new and strange, yet so as not to mislead. Conceding that he used this word figuratively, we are obliged to seek the application and meaning of the figure, not in the usages of the Old Testament, but in his own language. His meaning is found not in the literal meaning of the word in his own day or in the days of the prophets, but in his own use and application of the term. If he used the word figuratively with reference to the *finale* of a life of sin, and thereby made the valley of Hinnom, with all its horrors, the emblem of the punishment of the wicked after death, it makes no difference to the argument whether it had ever been so used before or not.

But here is another loose statement in this Catechism. It is intimated that we can select the sense to be attached to this word. We may understand it "either literally or figuratively!" Can this be so? Surely this author is wide of the mark here. The word must be taken literally or figuratively. It can not be both. The sense is too widely different. We must take it according to the facts. If Christ used this word literally, and meant by it just what is the literal meaning of the word, we dare not go beyond this and give it a figurative meaning. The assumption that he used it in the literal sense estops us from further inquiry concerning its emblematical meaning. On the other hand, if he did not use it with reference to its literal meaning, we are not bound by its literal meaning, whether in the days of Christ or of the prophets. This Catechism dodges the real issue by refusing to decide definitely whether we are bound to take the word literally or figuratively; and this is not an unusual thing with this class of expositors. They often find it convenient to alternate from the literal to the figurative according to the demands of the occasion; and when they adopt the figurative, they satisfy themselves too easily without tracing the figure to its application, or fixing upon it any definite meaning. This practice is reprehensible, in that it reduces the parables of the New Testament to the character of riddles, and puts the plain utterances of Christ on a level with pagan oracles. Figurative language is not necessarily ambiguous. Its meaning is as definite and as easily traced as is the most literal statement, and its interpretation requires no less positive rules than the other. To say of any word or phrase, "Oh, it is figurative; it may mean this, or it may mean that," is quite too common, but it is by no means satisfactory. But the author of this Catechism elsewhere admits that the Jews, at the time of Christ, had fallen into belief in the doctrine of eternal punishment, which he calls "the pagan dogma of eternal torture;" then, why not at once acknowledge the most natural thing in the world, that they were accustomed to regard the literal *Gehenna* as the emblem of that punishment? If the Jews believed this doctrine at all, as nearly all respectable Universalists admit they did, they believed that the Old Testament authorized it, and they used *Gehenna* to express it. It matters not, so far as this point is concerned, whence they derived this belief—whether they imbibed it from heathen sources or received it by tradition from their fathers or gathered it directly from the Scriptures—their faith in it proves that they believed their Scriptures warranted it, and their understanding of the words of Christ would be equally affected by their belief, whether that belief rested upon one foundation or another. We come, therefore, to the inquiry whether the Jewish people in the days of Christ believed in eternal punishment or not. If they did, the sense in which *Gehenna* occurs in the New Testament is settled in favor of the proposition we affirm; namely, that it means the last calamity of the wicked, the *finale* of a life of folly and crime.

Chapter X.

THE JEWISH BELIEF.

THE best way to learn the opinions of a people at a given time in their history, is to study their literature at the period in question, or as near to it as is possible. It is, however, conceded that there is no great amount of Jewish writing extant and now accessible which was unquestionably produced in the days of Christ and the apostles. Josephus and other Jewish writers of that age record, with great minuteness and general accuracy, the history of that nation, recounting their struggles, their oppressions, and their victories and defeats; but these records do not reveal with much clearness their mental conceptions of philosophy and religion. The discourse of Josephus concerning *Hades*, which is published as a part of his works, treats upon the subject in hand, and would be of great value, if its genuineness were incontestably established; but this is not the case. There are grave doubts whether it was written by Josephus. We do not, therefore, appeal to it as the language of the Jewish historian, nor do we place much dependence upon it as an authority for the particular shading of Jewish sentiment; but even though marks of a Christian paternity be traceable in it, its unquestionable antiquity, and the manifest purpose of the writer, whoever he was, to represent Jewish ideas, and his evident competency, give to the discourse sufficient weight to impose the burden of proof upon those who assert that it falsely attributes to the Jews opinions which they did not hold. According to this writer the Jews believed in a judgment after death, followed by eternal punishment to the wicked. It is evident that at the age in which this document was written intelligent Christians so understood the Jews and so represented them, and, so far as we can learn, without complaint or contradiction.

Josephus does, however, tell us that the Pharisees held "that all souls are incorruptible, but the souls of good men are only removed into other bodies, while the souls of bad men are subject to eternal punishment." (Wars of the Jews, II, 8, 14.) Again: "For the opinion obtains among them that bodies indeed are corruptible, and the matter of them not permanent, but that souls continue exempt from death forever; and that, emanating from the most subtile ether, they are enfolded in bodies as prisons, to which they are drawn by some natural spell. But when loosed from the bonds of the flesh, as if released from a long captivity, they rejoice and are borne upward. In this opinion, harmonizing with the sons of Greece, they maintain that virtuous souls have their habitation beyond the ocean, in a region oppressed neither with rains nor snows nor heats, but which the ever gentle zephyr refreshes, breathing from the wave; while to the bad they allot a gloomy and tempestuous cavern, full of never-ending punishments. According to the same notion, the Greeks seem to me to apportion to the brave, whom they style heroes and demigods, the islands of the blessed; but to the souls of the wicked, the place of the impious in *Hades*, where their legends tell that certain persons are punished, as Sisyphus, and Tantalus, and Tityus, laying it down, first, that souls are immortal, and deriving from thence their exhortations to virtue, and their dissuasives from vice." (Jewish War, II, 8, 10, 11.)

The Targums are perhaps the most authoritative expositions of Jewish faith, as it was when Christ was on earth, now within our reach. These afford unmistakable evidence that eternal punishment was taught and believed by the Jewish people. But the Targums are rarely seen or read by Christian people, and a few general remarks in relation to them will be in place. The following is from Horne's Introduction, and agrees with the most learned opinions on the subject: "The Chaldee word Targum signifies, in general, any version or explanation; but this appellation is more particularly restricted to the versions or paraphrases of the Old Testament, executed in the East Aramæan or Chaldee dialect, as it is usually called. These Targums are termed paraphrases or expositions, because they are rather comments and explications, than literal translations of the text; so that when the law was 'read in the synagogue every Sabbath-day,' in pure Biblical Hebrew, an explanation was subjoined to it in Chaldee, in order to render it intelligible to the people, who had but an imperfect knowledge of the Hebrew language. This practice, as already observed, originated with Ezra. As there are no traces of any written Targums prior to those of Onkelos and Jonathan, who are supposed to have lived about the time of our Savior, it is highly probable that these paraphrases were at first merely oral; that subsequently the ordinary glosses on the more difficult passages were committed to writing, and that as the Jews were bound by an ordinance of their elders to possess a copy of the law, these glosses were either afterwards collected together and deficiencies in them supplied, or new and connected paraphrases were formed." The Targums were evidently a growth. They contain the thought of the leaders of the people as taught in the synagogues, and unquestionably reveal the prevalent opinions of the Jews at the time of Christ and prior to his day. There are ten of them, on different parts of the Scriptures, written at different times and by different men, but when collected they form a continuous paraphrase on nearly all of the Old Testament. In regard to the light they shed on the particular subject in hand, I quote the learned Dr. Whitby—not as an authority upon the main issue, but as a capable and trustworthy witness to a fact; and the fact to be established is, that the Jews themselves did use this word with reference to future punishment, according to the testimony of the Targums.

Dr. Whitby says: "It seems reasonable to interpret them [words rendered Hell] according to the received opinion of the Jews, since otherwise our Lord's using them so frequently in speaking to them, without saying any thing to show that he did not understand the expression as they did, must have strengthened them in their error. Now it is certain that *Gehenna* (Hell) was still looked on as a place in which the wicked were to be tormented by fire. So the Jerusalem Targum, on Gen. xv, 17, represents it as sparkling and flaming with fire, into which the wicked fall. And the Targum upon Eccl.

ix, 15, speaks of the fire of Hell; and chapter x, 11, of the sparks of the fire of Hell; and chapter viii, 10, of the wicked who shall go to be burned in Hell."

The Doctor goes on to show from the similarity of the language of the Jews in the Targums to the expressions of our Lord with reference to *Gehenna*, that they would and did understand him as using that term with reference to punishment in the future state. The argument is conclusive; and the efforts of the opposition to break its force, or to obviate the conclusion to which it leads, so far from proving effective, tend rather to strengthen the conviction that it is unanswerable. There is in fact no answer to it, unless it can be shown that its foundation is false—that the Jews did not believe in eternal punishment, and needed to be taught it as a new doctrine, contrary to their previous ideas, in order to apprehend or believe it.

Dr. Adam Clarke tells us that the Targum on Isaiah xxxiii, 14, is as follows: "The sinners in Zion are broken down; fear hath seized the ungodly, who are suffering for their ways. They say, Who among us shall dwell in Zion, where the splendor of the Divine Majesty is like a consuming fire? Who of us shall dwell in Jerusalem, where the ungodly are judged and delivered into hell for an eternal burning?"

But those who assail the doctrine are not so ready to assail the foundation of this argument. They only seek to cast doubt upon it, or to leave it involved in uncertainty, so as to weaken any inferences that may be drawn from premises which are not well understood in all their relations. The cautiousness of their movements is accounted for by the fact that the most learned among them admit the main point in the case—that the Jews did, on some ground or other, believe that the wicked were destined to perish forever. They do, however, seek to obscure the argument, so far as it rests upon the Targums, by questioning the authority of these writings as containing the opinions of the Jews at the time of Christ. The Targums, as we have seen, contain the glosses or explanations which the Jewish teachers made upon the books of the Old Testament, after the mass of the people had lost the accurate knowledge of the Hebrew tongue in the Babylonian captivity. These expositions were first made orally, soon after the return of the Jews from Babylon; and they were passed down from one generation to another, in the teachings of the synagogues, until they were finally committed to writing with great care, so that they might be preserved in their purity for the benefit of all the Jews, scattered among the nations of the earth. Then, when we remember how strongly the Jews were attached to the opinions of their fathers, and how carefully they preserved their traditions, regarding them as sacred, the date of the written Targums will form no solid objection to the representations they make of the faith of the Jews, or rather to the application of that representation to the time Christ was on earth, even if it should turn out that they were not written till after the destruction of Jerusalem and the dispersion that followed. There is no evidence that the Jews changed their belief in regard to future punishment, or with reference to any of their great doctrines, between the days of Christ and the writing of the Targums; so that there is no ground whatever for doubting that these writings faithfully set forth the belief of the Jews at the beginning of the Christian era. The best authority fixes the date of the Jerusalem Targum near the close of the second century; but the force of the argument would scarcely be weakened if we should concede to it even a later origin. The thoughts it embodies were the thoughts of the generations past, grown sacred by the lapse of years.

Our opponents seek further to weaken the argument from the belief of the Jews, by keeping prominent the errors into which they had fallen, and the influences that operated to lead them into heretical notions. We concede that the Jews were not the best teachers in philosophy or religion, and that in many things they were both blind and obstinate; but this is not the pertinent fact. We do not believe in future punishment because the Jews did, nor are we concerned about the ground of their faith. The adversaries of this doctrine, the most intelligent of them, admit the fact that the Jews believed in the "dogma of eternal punishment," and then enlarge on the errors and superstition of the times, the absurdities of Jewish traditions, and their near resemblance to pagan philosophy; in all which they overlook the real issue, in that we do not hold that the doctrine is true because the Jews thought it true, nor for the reasons that induced them to accept it, but simply because our Savior found them believing it, and did not contradict them, or in any way manifest dissent from the prevailing notion. The corruption of their faith, their superstition, their blindness, and the influence of pagan philosophy on their beliefs, have nothing to do with the point in hand. The question is, Did the Jews believe the doctrine, and did Christ fail to correct them by teaching a different doctrine?

Finding it impossible to deny the fact, Universalists assert that the Jews learned their notions of Hell from heathen sources; that they abandoned the cherished teachings of their ancestors and the sacred writings of their prophets for the silly inventions of pagan philosophers and the dreams of mythology; and that Jesus Christ just repeated the popular notions of the people, without any protest against them as errors or against

THE JEWISH BELIEF. 177

their heathen origin. They tell us, as in the language of Dr. Williamson, in regard to *Hades*, that "our Savior fitted his discourse to his hearers," and "founded his parable precisely upon their views;" and yet they do not pretend to point out any contradiction he ever made to this popular notion, or any rebuke he ever administered to any one for believing in eternal punishment. What is all this better than to assert that Jesus was an impostor, and that the New Testament is a compilation of heathen fables?

Mr. Weaver says: "A future Hell was not taught in the Old Testament, nor known to the Jews as a Scripture teaching; but only as a sentiment which they had learned of the heathen." He then asserts that Christ used the word in a Scripture sense, and not in a heathen sense. The baseless assumption that the Jews understood the prevailing opinion respecting Hell to be of heathen origin, and contrary to the Scriptures, is the foundation of his effort to break the fact that the Jews believed in Hell, and that Christ did not contradict them. He says, further: "If he [Christ] had given to it a new sense, or a heathen sense, he would have told them of it. But as he used it without any explanation, we are left to the unavoidable conclusion that he used it in the Scriptural sense which all the Jews understood." (See Bible View, p. 70.) Here is the important admission that Christ used the word "without any explanation," and therefore in the sense "which all the Jews understood." But if so, "we are left to the unavoidable conclusion" that he sanctioned what the Jews believed. Mr. Weaver's mistake lies in the assumption that the Jews distinguished between the Scripture sense of the word and the sense or sentiment they had learned of the heathen. There is not the least shadow of authority for this. The Jews not only knew of the doctrine of eternal punishment in Hell, but they believed it; and they believed it not merely as a heathen sentiment, or on the authority of pagan philosophy, but as a divine revelation through their sacred books, and sanctioned by the traditions taught in their synagogues. They were the last people in the world to borrow doctrines from their heathen neighbors, in opposition to their own Scriptures.

THE JEWISH BELIEF.

If this doctrine was of heathen origin, and contrary to the Scriptures, the Jews neither knew nor believed the fact. They were not in the habit of receiving their doctrines from heathen sources, consciously at least, and if they did so in this instance, they would not have discriminated between the source of this and other doctrines held by them so as to say, This is of heathen origin and that is from the Holy Scriptures. And if they were deceived in this matter, and deceiving others, supposing this part of their faith to be of divine origin and derived from the Scriptures when it was not, the Savior was bound, as a divine teacher, to break the delusion, by explaining the source of the error, and denouncing the heresy. Silence would have been criminal. But the Savior was not silent; neither did he denounce the error. He made no reference to the heathen origin of the dogma of eternal punishment in *Gehenna*. On the contrary, he used the same terms, and the same symbols, which the Jews employed to express their ideas of eternal punishment, and he applied them in the same way, only with greater emphasis, to express the "oppressive and dreadful judgments" that should befall the wicked as "the *finale* of human folly and crime." From all which the conclusion is inevitable that Christ found no fault with the Jews respecting their belief in the final punishment of the wicked, but sanctioned their belief in all essential particulars.

We say in all essential particulars, for it is well known that the Jews indulged in many fancies in regard to the location of Hell, and the nature of its torments, which, in the light of modern intelligence, are quite preposterous. While he did not explain their errors in philosophy, or their absurd conjectures in relation to incidental and minor points, he did not sanction them, as they were not included in the terms he employed, nor did they constitute the really important part of the Jewish belief. He sanctioned that which he affirmed, and nothing more.

Chapter XI.

GEHENNA—SCRIPTURE USE.

We come now to the passages of Scripture in which *Gehenna* occurs, and while it may not be necessary to examine critically every instance of its use, we shall omit none that sheds light on the question in issue. The only object is to reach the precise meaning of the word as intended by the Great Teacher.

The first passage to be considered is Matt. v, 21, 22: "Ye have heard that it was said by them of old time, Thou shalt not kill; and whosoever shall kill shall be in danger of the judgment: but I say unto you, that whosoever is angry with his brother without cause shall be in danger of the judgment; and whosoever shall say to his brother, Raca, shall be in danger of the council; but whosoever shall say, Thou fool, shall be in danger of

Gehenna—fire." Here are three offenses specified—causeless anger, contemptuous speeches, and abusive epithets; and corresponding to these, three grades or degrees of punishment are indicated; namely, the judgment, the council, and the fire of *Gehenna*. Now the first question that arises is, Are these things to be taken literally, or must they be interpreted in a figurative sense? If they are to be taken literally, the Savior did nothing more than point out the punishments inflicted by the civil courts of the nation. But this view can not be accepted for many reasons, among which are the following:

1. There is no evidence that punishment by burning in the valley of Hinnom was practiced in the days of Christ, or that it had been for a long time before.

2. The offenses specified are not such as would expose those guilty of them to the several degrees of punishment here indicated. These punishments were strangling, stoning, and burning—all capital; but the Jewish courts inflicted none of these for the offenses mentioned. Indeed there is no evidence that such offenses came under the cognizance of

the law in any way, or incurred any penalty whatever.

3. The Savior was not speaking of punishments to be inflicted under the law of the land. So far from this, he distinguished between the crimes and punishments under the Jewish law, and those about which he was speaking, so as to mark the difference and show the contrast. He may have alluded to the regulations of the law when he said, "Ye have heard that it was said by them of old time," as the Jews largely conformed their statutes to the traditions received from "them of old time;" but when he added with emphasis, *"But I say unto you,"* he directed attention to something the courts did not condemn or punish.

4. Christ had no authority under the law to say who should or who should not be held amenable to the secular courts, and he never attempted to legislate or judge in regard to such matters. When, on one occasion, he was solicited to do something of this nature, he rebuked the applicant sharply, saying, "Man, who made me a judge or divider over you?" He utterly disclaimed all

right or purpose to meddle with the law of the land or with the functions of the courts. But in this emphatic "I say unto you," he asserted his right and authority over the matters in hand; and therefore we must suppose him to be speaking of spiritual things, and of such matters of offense and punishment as came under his jurisdiction as king in Zion.

With all his anxiety to get rid of punishment in the future world, Mr. Weaver rejects this interpretation as "too literal." One thing is certain, however, and that is, we must accept the passage as entirely literal, or abandon the literal sense altogether. He says, "This makes the passage too literal to meet my views of the Savior's teaching. It is very probable that he wished to warn his disciples against the dangers with which they were beset, and alluded to the horrible end of Jewish wickedness, by reference to the fire of *Gehenna*. But it is clear to my mind that these punishments of the Jewish code are made emblematic of God's spiritual punishments, teaching that as the Jews punished their transgressors according to the degree of guilt, so God would be equally just. Every offense should meet its merited penalty." (Bible View, page 75.) No serious objection need be urged against this statement, as far as it goes; for it accepts the essential point that the literal punishments of the Jewish code are emblematical of God's spiritual punishments. This carries the whole subject of the offenses and punishments over into the spiritual realm, where Christ is judge and dispenser of retributions. It therefore leaves the further application of Mr. Weaver's idea of spiritual punishment in the mists of confusion and unauthorized conjecture; for he applies this expressive phrase to the national calamities that came on the Jews in this world. We accept the statement that *Gehenna* is the emblem of "spiritual punishments;" but when this author undertakes to restrict those spiritual punishments to this life, and to make them all reformatory in character, he departs from authority and consistency as well. For it is well known that not only does this writer, but all others of the class to which he belongs, in seeking after the "spiritual punishments" emblematically set forth under the language in question, find them in the national overthrow of the Jews at the time Jerusalem was destroyed—punishments of a singular type as to spiritual qualities or reformatory tendencies.

There is no reasonable doubt that this passage is to be interpreted as relating to spiritual things, and that the terms judgment, council, and *Gehenna* are to be understood as metaphors, pointing to spiritual punishments. But on this very account, as well as for other reasons, it is improper to understand *Gehenna* as denoting the national calamity which has been made to figure so largely in the discussion of future punishment. Against any interpretation that makes *Gehenna* in any way express the overthrow of the Jewish nation, or apply to national disaster, the following objections appear to me to be conclusive:

1. The offenses and punishments spoken of in this passage are clearly of individual, and not of national character. Ill tempers and abusive speeches are the offenses. These are hinderances to spiritual life, and if cherished or persisted in will imperil the soul, because they stand in the way of inward purity and of unselfish consecration; but these are not the

great national crimes that brought the divine vengeance upon the devoted people, in the destruction of their temple and city, and in the subversion of their national polity. Doubtless, if the Savior, in his sermon on the mount, had desired to be understood as speaking of that coming wrath upon the nation, he would have mentioned some of the offenses which had become national, and which were leading to that consummation.

2. In the national retribution which followed the national rejection of the Messiah, there was nothing answering to the grades of punishment indicated by the terms judgment, council, and *Gehenna;* nor was that great calamity the result of any judicial proceeding, or of a sentence pronounced in any council or any court. And just here it may be well to correct a misstatement found in the "Bible View," and which is often made by those who deny the finality of future punishment. Mr. Weaver says: "The common doctrine is that there are no degrees of guilt; but all impenitent offenders, from him who steals a pin to him who murders a nation, shall suffer an eternity of equal torment." (Bible View,

page 75.) The common doctrine is widely different from this. It does not enter into the secrets of the divine plans, and unfold all the mystery of God's methods of dealing with the incorrigible, but it does affirm that in the final adjustment each and all will receive according to the deeds done in the body. It therefore affirms degrees of punishment in eternity, and we dare not doubt that God can punish men in the future according to the degrees of their guilt, as well as in this world. Duration is only one element in the retribution of sin, and a consequential and not a primary element at that.

3. The context shows that Christ was here giving directions for the regulation of personal conduct, and particularly personal tempers and passions, in all succeeding ages, and stating the consequences of disregarding the direction given, not only to the Jews, but to all people; not only at that time, but in all time. The language, therefore, applies to men during the whole period of the Gospel dispensation. It is a statute law in the Church or kingdom of Christ on earth, unrepealed and unrepealable forever; whereas, if

it related to the national punishment of the Jews in the destruction of Jerusalem, it could only interest those who lived prior to that wonderful event.

4. It will not do to make *Gehenna* point to the national overthrow of the Jews, and the judgment and council to minor offenses and punishments of a personal kind. If the passage is figurative, it is all figurative. If *Gehenna* is an emblem, so are the different courts alluded to. If one term relates to national affairs, so must all the others. But while liberalists of almost every school have insisted on applying *Gehenna* as an emblem of national punishments, they have uniformly failed to make application of the other terms to any thing that ever took place on the earth. The truth is, the Savior, while discoursing of spiritual offenses, as contrasted with mere overt acts of disobedience to the law, alluded to the council and judgment and *Gehenna-fire* for the purpose of impressing the hearer with the reality of those offenses, and the severity of divine punishments, as compared with those which were external and temporary. He also designed, undoubtedly, to intimate the gen-

eral fact that there are degrees of punishment in the future state, corresponding to the different measures of ill-desert, according to the judgment and counsel of infinite wisdom; and, finding no words in the language of the people, through which he could convey his ideas of the spiritual state without the use of metaphors, he illustrated the whole subject by this reference to the Jewish courts.

It is a very important rule for the interpretation of figurative language that requires us to avoid extending the comparison in the metaphor beyond the point of resemblance that suggested its use. The observance of this rule will lead us to accept the above statement as sufficient, and prevent us from the fruitless labor of seeking a multitude of correspondences between the literal and spiritual in this passage, where only a single one was intended. If we have gathered the great thought of the Master in regard to sins of the heart, and the adjustment of punishment in the future state according to the grades of guilt, we have a sufficient explanation of the metaphors used, and will do wrong to press those metaphors to yield the details of mode and method and result, which it might be gratifying to understand, but which they were never intended to exhibit.

The author of the "Bible View of Hell" makes an objection to the application of *Gehenna* to the future state, which deserves notice here. It is that "the difference between the sinfulness of saying Raca or blockhead and fool, is hardly great enough to warrant such a difference in punishment as is involved in the supposition" that *Gehenna-fire* is in the future. His difficulty arises from his confusion or misconception of the case. He takes it for granted that we concede, or are obliged to consider the punishments of the first and second offenses as the inflictions of the Jewish courts, or as necessarily in this life, and temporal. But we do nothing of the kind. The sins are all of the heart, and the punishments are all spiritual, and the whole scene of retribution is in eternity, not in time. This writer adds, "There is no proportion between the slight difference in guilt and the tremendous difference in punishment." If we should allow him to make part of the text literal and part figurative, and part of the punishments temporal and part spiritual, there might be found something like his wide difference and his tremendous disproportion; but this is almost unpardonable blundering. The passage is all figurative, and none of the punishments were to be inflicted by the courts, and none of the offenses were to be estimated by their outward manifestations or external differences. If the passage is not figurative, it is not true; for the courts neither strangled nor stoned men for saying "blockhead," any more than they burned them literally in the valley of Hinnom for saying "thou fool." We must be consistent and admit metaphors where they exist, and yet not force them to crawl where they are evidently intended to stand still. And as the metaphors express spiritual punishments, so the offenses named stand for the inward dispositions out of which they spring, and which are the real cause of the severities described. The scope of this whole discourse proves this, as its great aim was to turn attention to the spirituality of the divine law, which applies to the thoughts of the heart as well as to the actions of the life.

Chapter XII.

GEHENNA—SCRIPTURE USE, CONTINUED.

THE next occurrence of *Gehenna* is in a passage which is one of a class, similar language being used by our Savior on different occasions. Instead of considering each separately, we will group these Scriptures, and gather from the whole the precise meaning of this word, as it was employed in these remarkable discourses. "And if thy right eye offend thee, pluck it out, and cast it from thee: for it is profitable for thee that one of thy members should perish, and not that thy whole body should be cast into *Gehenna*. And if thy right hand offend thee, cut it off, and cast it from thee; for it is profitable for thee that one of thy members should perish, and not that thy whole body should be cast into *Gehenna*." (Matt. v, 29, 30.) See also Matthew xviii, 8, 9, where occur the phrases "everlasting fire" and *Gehenna-fire*, as enlargements on the simple word *Gehenna*. Also Mark ix, 43-48: "And if thy hand offend thee, cut it off: it is better for thee to enter into life maimed, than having two hands to go into *Gehenna*, into the fire that never shall be quenched; where their worm dieth not, and the fire is not quenched. And if thy foot offend thee, cut it off: it is better for thee to enter halt into life, than having two feet to be cast into *Gehenna*, into the fire that never shall be quenched; where their worm dieth not, and the fire is not quenched. And if thine eye offend thee, pluck it out: it is better for thee to enter into the kingdom of God with one eye, than having two eyes, to be cast into *Gehenna-fire:* where their worm dieth not, and the fire is not quenched."

There will probably be no doubt in any one's mind that "*Gehenna*," "*Gehenna-fire*," "everlasting fire," and "the fire that never shall be quenched," relate to the same thing, and that the varied expressions emphasize the thought expressed by the single word *Gehenna*. These varied expressions bring out different phases of the punishment of *Gehenna* and mark the scope and applicatian of that word. On the other hand, the two phrases "enter into life" and "enter into the kingdom of God" mean the same thing, and show us the opposite of entering into *Gehenna*. In all these Scriptures there are two, and only two, opposite states described. Men do not "go into *Gehenna*" and also "enter into life." The one state precludes or cuts off the other. Then, in view of the liberalistic interpretations of these passages making *Gehenna* an emblem of the destruction of Jerusalem, as well as claiming that it expresses literal punishments under the laws of the nation, the following question arises for consideration: Can these Scriptures be understood either literally of the punishments inflicted by Jewish courts in the valley of Hinnom; or figuratively of the national overthrow of the Jews, in the destruction of their temple and city?

Neither of these interpretations can be sustained, and of course they can not both be true. All the reasons why the passage considered in the preceding chapter could not be so interpreted, apply with equal force to those now before us. There is no evidence that punishment by burning in the valley of Hinnom was lawful when these words were spoken; if it was lawful there are no crimes mentioned that would expose any one to it; and he who uttered these words was not the judge in such matters, and was not defining the secular law, nor predicting the action of Jewish courts. Neither was he speaking of offenses of a national character, but of those that were personal; and although the degrees of punishment are not illustrated or recognized, as in the former instance, the language was evidently intended for universal application, and should not be restricted to Judea, nor to the period prior to the destruction of Jerusalem. It is a permanent law of the kingdom of God, applicable to the Church in all the world, and through all the ages, fixing the terms of discipleship, and proclaiming every-where and to all people the absolute indispensableness of self-denial. The sentiment is plain, and easily comprehended and applied. It is that if any one will not deny himself of all sinful gratifications, though it require a sacrifice as dear or as painful as the cutting off of a hand or a foot, or the plucking out of an eye, he shall not enter into life eternal in the kingdom of God, but on the contrary he shall be cast into *Gehenna*—"into the fire that shall never be quenched," "where their worm dieth not, and the fire is not quenched." This is the final doom of the wicked. So far as revelation is concerned, no ray of light gleams from beyond the eternal burnings; and it must not be forgotten for a moment that our inquiry is with reference to the voice of God in his written Word. We are not looking for the wherefore, nor for the result of this fire; nor yet for its locality, or its material or moral relations. The point in view is the simple fact that these Scriptures, in harmony with the tenor of divine teaching, point to an "everlasting fire" as the result of sinful living, to the rejection of Christ and his salvation. A few reflections will confirm this interpretation.

1. The "life" mentioned in these Scriptures is the opposite of *Gehenna*. To go or be cast into *Gehenna*, is to lose this "life;" and to "enter into life" is to escape *Gehenna*. Theologians of liberalistic views have

both seen and felt the force of this fact, and have endeavored to obviate it—possibly to their own satisfaction; but they have never removed the difficulty. In this interest we have been told that the "life" is spiritual; that it is enjoyed on earth, and that, therefore, it does not necessitate an interpretation that would carry the opposite conditions of humanity, described as "entering into life," on one hand, or "going into *Gehenna*," on the other, over into eternity for their realization. But spiritual life—that which comes to the soul by faith in Jesus Christ—is not the opposite of burning to death in the valley of Hinnom, nor of any physical torture or punishment whatsoever; neither is it, in any intelligible sense, the opposite of the national calamity of the Jews. The real antithesis to the life of faith is the spiritual death out of which the soul emerges when it "passes from death unto life," in conversion.

2. It is clearly impossible for any one to "enter into life," in the sense of these passages, and yet be "cast into *Gehenna*." But if the "life" is nothing more than the life of faith on the earth, there is no such impos-

sibility in the case; for it was clearly possible for believers, in the full enjoyment of spiritual life, to suffer any temporal calamity or judgment the word might import, and if the allusion was to such tortures as the courts might inflict the disciples of Christ were quite as liable to them as any other class of people. Spiritual life is not a protection against physical suffering, especially in such seasons of bitter persecution as followed the first preaching of the Gospel of Christ. And so, also, if the life is allowed to be eternal, and to pertain strictly to the immortal state, as it undoubtedly does, a person might be cast into *Gehenna*, literally, and burn to death, or suffer any temporal calamity the word may be supposed to indicate, if it be only temporal, and "then enter into life," in the eternal kingdom, just as readily and triumphantly as if no *Gehenna* had stood in the way. All such interpretations as make the *Gehenna* a temporary calamity, whether it be taken literally or figuratively, or made to represent personal or national experiences, will destroy the antithesis and break up the opposition between the states or conditions contemplated.

3. Self-denial is here enjoined as the safeguard, and as the only safeguard, against the fire of *Gehenna*. But self-denial did not save the first Christians from the most relentless persecutions. Many of them passed through "fiery trials" equal to any temporal calamity *Gehenna* could symbolize. They were brought before governors and kings, councils and courts, and were imprisoned, beheaded, stoned, sawn asunder, and burned; so that if *Gehenna* means "temporal calamities and distresses," these humble followers of Christ passed through its hottest burnings, in spite of their self-denial and faithfulness. On the other hand, both prior to the destruction of Jerusalem and since that event, multitudes have refused to practice self-denial, and yet have neither been burned in the valley of Hinnom, nor suffered any temporal calamity.

4. If we literalize *Gehenna*, so as to confine its application to the Jews, we should literalize the other parts of the passages, even to the cutting off of the hand and the foot and the plucking out of the eye. Perhaps no one will insist upon this; but why

not? Did not Christ speak as definitely and as positively of the body, and of maiming the body, as he did of *Gehenna?* Then why take the latter so literally as to apply it only to this world and to the Jews, and not do the same for the other expressions? But if it be true that the plucking out of the eye is a figurative expression, signifying rigid and painful self-denial, so also is it true that *Gehenna* is a figurative term, a metaphor, signifying that extreme punishment which must ultimately overtake the self-indulgent sinner. This is enough. The great thought of the Redeemer is brought out, and its importance justifies the repetition, which is so inexplicable on other grounds.

In addition to all this, it might be easily shown that our "liberalistic" friends do not entertain such high conceptions of spiritual life on earth, as that the rigid self-denial here contemplated is essential to the attainment of it. There is in the so-called liberalism of the times but little demand for cutting off hands or feet or plucking out offending eyes, and certainly not as conditions precedent to the life of faith which that system holds up as the best attainment in spiritual freedom. But the truth is, the "life" mentioned in these Scriptures as the opposite of *Gehenna*, is not a life that belongs to this world. It is a life beyond the mortal state, beyond the domain of sin and death; a life which *Gehenna* can not destroy, because it is not entered till all danger of "the fire that shall never be quenched" is past forever. It is the life reached by walking in the "narrow way." (Matt. vii, 13, 14.) This "walk" is to continue till the need of self-denial is over, and then introduce the pilgrim into the life which is beyond. It is the Christian's life on earth, the life of self-denial and cross-bearing which covers the existence here, and closes only with the close of probation. The life to which it "leads" is the goal of this; and as it is at the termination of the "narrow way," it is necessarily beyond the grave. The life of faith is entered not at the close but at the beginning of the life of self-denial. This is the inspiration of the walk in the narrow way. It links itself with cross-bearing. It is the power that strikes off the offending member, and gathers strength by the self-denial it demands and prompts. The way is so "narrow" that every evil desire and unholy impulse, every constitutional or besetting sin, must be conquered in order that we may keep in it. And it "leadeth unto life." That life crowns the struggling soul. The reverse of this is a dark picture. It is a "broad way"—a way broad enough to admit the whole brood of sensual delights. It requires no self-denying care, no cross-bearing, no conflict with self; but it "leadeth to destruction." This is the opposite of life, the synonym of *Gehenna*. Turn as we may, we are compelled to face the unavoidable conclusion that the "life" which is entered as the result of self-denial, and the *Gehenna* which awaits the self-indulgent are both in the state beyond probation. It matters not that we do not see all the reasons why this particular word should be chosen to express the outcome of the life of sin, or why the imagery of the valley of Hinnom should picture the horrors of the retribution in store for the ungodly, the fact is before us—the stern, unyielding fact, which no dexterity of interpretation can change, and no power of criticism can destroy. Nor does it diminish the force of the fact that we are unable so to trace this imagery in its application to the spiritual state as to mark the exact significance of each of its parts, or to comprehend the nature of the punishment symbolized or the agencies of its infliction. It seems to accord with the wisdom of God that in this life we should know spiritual things only "in part." This is true of the good and of the heavenly state; and much more might we expect it to be so of the world of darkness and death. That which remains unrevealed would serve no practical purpose if made known. We are warned of the fact and hopelessness of perdition, and further light upon the dreadfulness of the condition of the lost would not increase the motive to obedience and purity of life. If the light which is in us be darkness, additional light would enhance the darkness.

Chapter XIII.

GEHENNA—SCRIPTURE USE, CONTINUED.

THE Scriptures we are now to examine are so definite in their statements and many-sided in their bearing on the subject in hand, that they may very properly be taken as the most explicit proofs of the position we have assumed. Their testimony is clear, pointed, decisive. Of course, it has been challenged, and earnest, persistent efforts have been made to counteract or nullify the influence of this testimony on the issue pending; so that we can not proceed without noticing what "liberalists" have said upon these Scriptures.

The following are the passages: "And fear not them that kill the body, but are not able to kill the soul; but rather fear him which is able to destroy both soul and body in *Gehenna*." (Matt. x, 28.) "And I say unto you, my friends, be not afraid of them that kill the body, and after that, have no more that they can do. But I will forewarn you whom ye shall fear; fear him which, after he hath killed, hath power to cast into *Gehenna;* yea, I say unto you, fear him." (Luke xii, 4, 5.)

The first point that strikes the reader of these passages is, that the casting into *Gehenna* takes place after death—after the body is killed. This alone sheds a flood of light upon the whole subject. It stands out as a fact, broad and palpable, confronting every caviler with the distinctness of its significance, and commanding attention by the directness of its assertion. And there is no possible evasion of this speaking fact. The death which it is "after," is the death of the body. "After that"—"after he hath killed;" after he hath killed the body. *Gehenna* is, therefore, after death. And the next point worthy of remark is, that "both soul and body" may be cast into *Gehenna*. This is full of meaning, as we shall see further along. It implies the resurrection, or the reunion of soul and body after death, and after the dissolution of the body in the grave, and the abiding of the soul in *Hades* until the day of final doom. That reunion will come, and then also will come the last calamity that shall befall the wicked, the *finale* of human folly and crime.

But we must hear the opposers of this doctrine, the "liberalists," whose sensitive natures are shocked at God's own truth, so that they must needs soften it to their liking, or disbelieve it outright. We shall look at specimens of their interpretations, enough to bring out all the points, and exhibit the strength of their opposition to the natural import of the language, and point out the incorrectness of their positions and the failure of their criticisms.

Their first aim is to strike at the meaning of the word "soul." The object of this is not always apparent, but since importance is attached to it we must not overlook what has been said. The following are the words of a distinguished advocate of Universalism, whose opposition to the doctrine of future punishment secured him a wide reputation, and the highest respect of his class: "It is plain, then, that this word soul, in this place, does mean the animal life, and not the immortal spirit. Now, I wish you to bear in mind this definition of the meaning of the term soul here, and we will inquire, What is meant by destroying both soul and body in Hell (*Gehenna*), and who have power to do this? 'And fear not them which kill the body'— those minor authorities which have power only to take the life—but 'fear him'—that power or tribunal that has not only power to kill the body, to destroy the animal life, but to burn the body in *Gehenna*. Now mark, these were minor authorities that had no authority over the body after the life was taken; they had power to condemn the individual to be stoned to death, to be strangled to death, or to take his life in any manner whereby the animal life might be destroyed. But here was a power that could burn the body, destroy both soul and body in this *Gehenna*—Hell. There are powers among us that can destroy the animal life. They can hang up the culprit and there let him rest. And, in addition, they can hand over the body to the surgeons for dissection. So there is a

destruction of both the animal life and of
the body. Well, thus it was with respect to
the Sanhedrim; they had power not only to
destroy the animal life, but to burn the body
in the valley of the son of Hinnom. Such,
my friends, is the meaning of this text; it
has no reference to the condition of the immortal spirit in the future world." So said
Mr. Doolittle, and multitudes of "liberalists"
have rejoiced in the genius which devised so
profound an exposition!

It is humiliating to feel obliged to make
serious answer to a statement so futile and
self-contradictory, and yet it is put forth as
real argument, and widely accepted as break-
ing the force of the testimony of these Scriptures in favor of the final perdition of the
wicked. Others may gloss the position with
finer rhetoric, burying the idea under a tor-
rent of words, but adding nothing to the
thought. The leading point is the definition
of the word "soul." It is said to mean the
"animal life." There is a purpose in this,
because the "soul" can be lost, and here it
appears capable of going into *Gehenna* after
the body is dead. But let us read the pas-

sage with this definition substituted for soul: "And fear not them that kill the body, but are not able to kill the animal life!" Every one sees the absurdity of this, because every one knows that the body can not be killed without destroying the animal life. But since there is a power that can kill the body without killing the soul, the word soul must mean something distinct from the body and distinct also from the animal life. It is true that in a few instances the word rendered soul in this place is rendered life, but never animal life. An example is found in John xii, 25: "He that loveth his life shall lose it; and he that hateth his life in this world, shall keep it unto life eternal." This teaches the necessity of self-denial here in order to obtain life eternal hereafter. But the word *pseuche*, rendered "life" in this place, and soul in the passages under consideration, is the proper word for soul, while *zoe* is the proper word for life. It is easily seen that *pseuche* is rendered life as a secondary or metaphorical meaning, in view of the fact that the soul remains with the body only while the life lasts. We are accustomed to speak of death, or the giving up of life, as the giving up of the soul. Popular thought and popular expression would have it that the soul animates the body, and is the life of the body, but this is neither physiologically nor theologically accurate. The soul survives the shock that prostrates the body to the dust, or the language of Christ is meaningless. Men are able to kill the body, but are not able to kill the soul.

The next point has reference to the object of fear, or rather to the person or power the disciples were forewarned to fear. Liberalists prefer not to believe that God is represented as a terror or dread to the wicked. They see in this sentiment possibilities of great hazard to their cherished notions. Hence, as in the above exposition, comparisons are made between minor and major authorities of the Jews. Some had limited power, and others unlimited; some could destroy the life, but could not destroy the body, while others could dispose of the body after it was dead. The disciples ought not, therefore, to be afraid of the minor authorities, but only of the Sanhedrim! Is not this trifling? And yet we encounter it as sober criticism, speaking for superior learning and advanced thought! In order to agree with this exposition, our Savior should have reversed his statement, and said, "Fear not them that kill the soul—the animal life—but are not able to dispose of the body after it is dead!"

But whom should we fear? Upon this point our "liberal" friends are not agreed, and therefore we shall have to notice more than one answer. As seen above, we are told it is the Sanhedrim, or great council of the Jews, which had power over the body after it was dead, and might burn it in the valley of Hinnom. The absurdity of this has already appeared; but, for the reason that much stress is often laid upon it, a little further attention to it must be indulged. The context is adduced with much confidence to show that the disciples were not to be afraid of God, who cared for the falling sparrow, and much more for them, but that they were to fear the Sanhedrim, whose power was so great that it could destroy the body after it was dead. But the context shows that Christ was sending forth his disciples to preach the kingdom of God, and giving them suitable instructions and encouragement for their mission, warning them of dangers to be encountered, and telling them how to conduct themselves. He told them of the persecutions they would meet, but they were not to desist from their work on account of any treatment they might receive at the hands of men. He said, "But beware of men; for they will deliver you up to the councils, and they will scourge you in their synagogues; and ye shall be brought before governors and kings for my sake, for a testimony against them and the Gentiles." Then, after explaining how they should answer their accusers, and expect divine assistance in their trials, he encouraged them as follows: "Fear them not therefore; for there is nothing covered that shall not be revealed; and hid that shall not be known. What I tell you in darkness, that speak ye in light; and what ye hear in the ear, that preach ye upon the housetops. And fear not them which kill the body, but are not able to kill the soul; but rather fear him which is able to destroy both soul and body in *Gehenna*. Are not two sparrows sold for a farthing?

and one of them shall not fall on the ground without your Father. But the very hairs of your head are all numbered. Fear ye not therefore; ye are of more value than many sparrows." These several expressions, "Beware of men," "Fear them not therefore," "Fear not them which kill the body," "Fear ye not therefore," all relate to earthly powers, including governors, kings, councils, Sanhedrim and all. The disciples were thus expressly commanded not to be afraid of any earthly power whatever, whether small or great, and for the reason that these powers could do nothing more than kill the body. There was one who could do more, and he was watching them and caring for them, and would be with them in all danger, but they must not offend him. It was better to die than to disobey God. They must therefore maintain their integrity in spite of kings and governors, in spite of councils and tortures, in spite of stoning or strangling or burning to death, whether in the valley of the son of Hinnom or anywhere else. They were even to hate their own lives in this world, that they might keep them unto life eternal in the world to come. What, then, in view of all this, induces men to assert that these disciples were to discriminate between earthly tribunals, and fear one only and not the others? If there is any meaning in the Savior's words, they are to be taken as encouragement not to fear any earthly power, but to commit soul and body to him who cares for sparrows, and numbers the hairs of the head, and is able to save the soul, even when the body perishes. Interpreted thus the language is pertinent and forcible.

But, as before intimated, this interpretation is not satisfactory to all "liberalists." Even Universalists attempt another. They sometimes admit that God was to be feared, because he was able to destroy both soul and body. But this, to them, is dangerous ground, and they step carefully upon it. The admission necessitates a different view of the entire passage, which we have in the language of T. B. Thayer, as follows: "If you are moved by the selfish consideration of fear to abandon the Gospel in order to save your lives (as Peter was afterward tempted to do), then to be consistent, you ought to fear the power which can do the most injury. And this surely is God, who can bring destruction and death not only on the body but on the soul also, and that amid the most terrible of judgments. And to picture the dreadfulness of this destruction more vividly to their minds, he uses the well-known symbol of *Gehenna*, or the valley of Hinnom, the synonym of all that was horrible in the mind of the Jew." (History of Endless Punishment, page 108.)

This paraphrase will do very well, if it be kept in mind that the destruction of soul and body, so vividly pictured to the mind by the familiar symbol of *Gehenna*, was after death; but this application Mr. Thayer omits. He insists that *Gehenna* symbolizes only temporal judgments, which, after all, could only kill the body, and could not kill the soul. But men could do this; and men were the agents in the very judgments which this author supposes to be intended. The destruction of Jerusalem was the work of men, though Providence permitted it, and used the evil passions of human hearts in accomplishing his own purposes. And in all that terrible siege and carnage, there was not a single agency that could destroy a soul after the body was killed.

Mr. Thayer virtually acknowledges the weakness of his statement at this point, and intimates that the Savior only mentioned a possible case—that God *could* destroy both soul and body after death, and therefore was to be feared, though there was not the slightest danger that he would do such a thing! He would have the Son of man, under these solemn circumstances, warning his disciples to peril their lives in his cause, and holding a scarecrow before them as an inspiration to fidelity! After admitting that the disciples were charged to fear God because he was able to destroy both soul and body, Mr. Thayer continues: "In the next words he proceeds to tell them that really they have no cause to fear either God or men." How is this? Did he conclude to withdraw the *brutum fulmen?* Had he not said, "I will forewarn you whom ye shall fear?" And had he not emphasized this, and made it a positive command by adding, "Yea, I say unto you, fear him?" Are we to believe that he did this, and then immediately turned round and told them that this was all a sham, a mere supposititious case, and that there was in reality no cause to fear either God or men? Verily this style of "liberal" exposition needs the charity that covers a multitude of sins.

But Mr. Thayer's next remark is a very good one: "So long as they did their duty, God, who provided for the sparrows, and numbered the hairs of their heads in the watchfulness of his love, would surely protect them." Yes, his unfluctuating love would not fail, and their devotion to duty would meet its reward, even though the body should fall, and life itself be given up. We would emphasize the first clause of Mr. Thayer's sentence, and give it cordial indorsement. But how crooked is error! His next sentence is most remarkable. It is this: "And then, as if to convince them that what he had said was only a supposition, and not a fact, he says, 'Fear ye not therefore; ye are of more value than many sparrows.'" The scarecrow theory is not abandoned. Truly, "so long as they did their duty," they need not be afraid of men; for the worst that could happen would not destroy the soul, but only kill the body, while he who cares for the sparrows would save them eternally. And "so long as they did their duty," they need not be afraid of God; their fear was not to take that form; for there was no danger that God would destroy them soul and body in *Gehenna* if they stood fast in their integrity. But how does this prove that what the Savior had been telling them was "supposition, and not a fact."

This attempt to make out that the allusion to the possible destruction of soul and body in Hell after death is "a supposition and not a fact"—a mere scarecrow—is a confession that the language of Christ, strictly interpreted in its most natural sense, does convey the idea of a final punishment after death, or in eternity. Else why hold that the real idea is a "supposition, and not a fact?" If the language meant simply a temporal calamity, no resort to the idea of a mere "supposition" would be thought of or cherished for a moment. Yes, here we have it at last—the culmination of liberalistic criticism—the doctrine of the eternal perdition of ungodly men is taught in the New Testament, but only as "a supposition, not as a fact!" But what influence upon the mind of the disciples are we to suppose this announcement would have, if accompanied by the assurance that the power to destroy the soul and body after death was only an idea, that it was a power which could never be exercised? To appeal to the existence of such a power was a mockery, if it was only a supposition. The argument runs thus: "Eternal punishment is a possibility; that is, God is able to inflict it, and appeal is made to this ability to inspire fear in the hearts of men; but, then, it must be distinctly understood that there is in reality no danger and no cause of fear!"

But this author is afraid of annihilation, and argues on this wise, in a note on page 106: "If it teaches what is certain, and not what is possible only, it necessitates the doctrine of annihilation." The supposed annihilation is in the word "destroy," and that word comes as near annihilation, and necessitates the doctrine just as much, if the *Gehenna* relates to mundane punishment, as if it symbolizes punishment after death. The destruction of soul and body is predicated as positively in one case as the other; and we do not understand that any claim is set up that temporal judgments are only suppositions. This writer is too "liberal;" he has overloaded his cannon, and falls under the rebound. In order to avoid "annihilationism," which he does not avoid, he represents the Savior as exhorting the disciples with one breath to fear God, because he is able to destroy them soul and body, and with the next breath trying to persuade them that they have no cause to fear either God or man! But to all unbiased minds, the very fact that the Savior told the disciples what God was able to do with them, as a reason why they should fear and obey him, is positive proof that there was danger of incurring that identical retribution.

But even this interpretation, this make-believe theory, fails to satisfy the enemies of the doctrine of eternal punishment; and so they have another. At all hazards they must escape the idea of punishment in *Gehenna* after death. If it were only the recognition of suffering in *Hades*, the case would not be so serious. They do admit that, and without fatal results, for they can fall back upon the ultimate destruction of *Hades*, when it shall deliver up its inhabitants, as it surely will, in the resurrection of the dead, and assert their restoration; but there is no destruction of *Gehenna*. The Bible is silent on that subject. Those "cast into *Gehenna*" do not come out again, so far as any hint is given. What then must be done? The language is plain, that whatever destruction in *Gehenna* means, it takes place after the body is killed; and we have all along supposed that killing the body meant death. We assume this, and proceed as if the position were uncontradicted, but it is not. Liberalists have discovered that it means nothing of the kind! To admit that to "kill the body" means the death of the body, would still leave the way open to conclude that the casting into *Gehenna*, after the body is killed, means a *Gehenna* after death. This would show that this terrible calamity relates to the future world— the very thing to be avoided.

But what can be meant by the word "kill"

in this wonderful Scripture, and by the phrase, "after he hath killed?" Rev. G. S. Weaver comes to the rescue here and tells us all about it. Hear him: "By the word 'kill' here he doubtless meant just what he did by the word 'scourge' a few verses before, when speaking of the same men." But then the disciples were not to be afraid of scourging; and if the word "kill" means scourge, it means the same when applied to the action of Him, who, after he hath scourged (killed), hath power to cast into *Gehenna*. But God did not scourge the bodies of men. And it would be difficult to find any who could "scourge" the body, but could not "scourge" the soul; and not less difficult to find who could scourge the body, and after that have "no more that they could do." But this astute critic, while searching the context for that word "scourge," used of these same men, might have found, a little nearer the text, too, the following: "And the brother shall deliver up the brother to death, and the father the child; and the children shall rise up against their parents, and cause them to be *put to death*." If Mr. Weaver was really anxious to find the meaning of the word "kill" by consulting the connection, why did he go back of this verse and select the word "scourge?" Does that word express all the persecutions to which the followers of Christ were liable? If so, putting to death means "scourging," and all the New Testament says of martyrdom is reduced to "scourging!" Such a defense ought to bring suspicion upon any doctrine.

But Mr. Weaver does not believe that God was to be feared because he was able to destroy both soul and body in *Gehenna* after death. Neither does he agree with his brethren who hold that the Sanhedrim was the power that was able to cast into *Gehenna* after the body was killed. He has discovered that the Jews, in our Savior's time, had no right to inflict capital punishment, they being subject to the Roman power. He therefore contends that the disciples were commanded not to fear the Jewish authorities, but to stand in awe of the Romans! Thus he paraphrases: "Fear not them which have power to scourge and torture the body, but have not power to take life; but rather fear him (the Roman governor) who has power to destroy life and body in *Gehenna.*" (Bible View of Hell, pp. 77, 78).

Unfotunately for this interpretation, the disciples had just been notified that they would be "scourged in the synagogues," and "be brought before governors and kings," and these they were not to fear. And inasmuch as there were no governors except Roman governors before whom they could be brought, they were positively commanded not to fear the Roman governor! They were to be arraigned by their own countrymen, the Jews, "for a testimony against them and the Gentiles;" and their zeal was not to abate even though they encountered the power of the Romans, or any earthly tribunal whatsoever. They were to endure scourging and torture, and to be "put to death" without flinching. They were to hate their own lives also, esteeming the love of Christ better than father, mother, wife, or children. But if so, what folly to claim that they were to fear the Roman power because it could kill them! This notion that the Roman governor was to be feared is useless without the definition of the word "kill," which has been shown to be without support and positively absurd.

Does the reader say to himself that these quibbles are too frivolous to deserve refutation? It seems to me that he must; and yet these very criticisms are made and these ridiculous positions assumed by learned men, leaders of public thought in the relentless warfare "liberalism" is making against the faith of the Church in regard to eternal retributions. Therefore nothing that bears on the meaning of these Scriptures, or on the positions of the parties to this controversy, should be deemed beneath our notice. My purpose has been to follow the tortuous course of "liberalistic" exposition far enough to reveal its animus, and to show the lengths to which the adversaries of the doctrine of future punishment will go, and the vagaries they will accept, rather than submit to the plain testimony of Christ. Such attempts to twist the meaning of these Scriptures reveal the stubbornness of the opposition, and proclaim its weakness.

The outcome of this inquiry is stated in few words. The Savior pointed his disciples to all the persecutions to which they would be exposed—to scourging, torture, and death, whether at the hands of Jews or Gentiles, whether by law or without law; and in full view of all that could be done to them by ferocious enemies, stirred to madness by furious passions, he told them to fear no earthly power which could kill the body, *and after that could do no more;* but to fear God, who, after he hath killed, can cast into *Gehenna.* What language could more positively declare a Hell beyond the grave?

But when the body is killed, the soul separates from it, and enters *Hades,* not *Gehenna,* while the body molders into dust. True, but "the end cometh," in the which the graves will give up the dead, and *death* and *Hades* will deliver up their dead, and then soul and body will be cast into *Gehenna.* Nothing harmonizes apparent discrepancies like the simple truth.

Chapter XIV.

THE LAKE OF FIRE.

THE next point in our inquiry reaches to the end of things. It takes us down the ages to the consummation. We must therefore deal with mysteries, and follow glimmerings of light, and, perchance, fragments of truth. Of course we move cautiously, but we may move, and we must. The symbols of revelation speak to us, and will be heard.

There is a "lake of fire"—at least this language is in the Bible, and it means something. Well for us if we give it the meaning with which the Holy Spirit has invested it! To do this we must not be wise above what is written, nor flinch from the results involved, however stern.

Gehenna is the theme. This is beyond death. Has it any connection with the "lake of fire?" My proposition is, *Gehenna*, as used by our Lord, represents the same punishment, the same state and doom of the wicked, that is symbolized in the "Apocalypse," by the "lake of fire," and the "second death."

This does not mean that *Gehenna* is an emblem of the lake of fire. Both are symbols. At least *Gehenna* is used metaphorically, the name of a literal valley on earth, passing over to a state or place of punishment in the future, of which identical punishment the lake of fire is a symbol. Each pictures to the mind the same outcome of the life of sin, the ultimate and irreversible perdition of ungodly men.

This proposition will not be seriously questioned by Universalists or liberalists of any school. Their opposition is to the application of the symbols. The necessities of their case oblige them to seek an application of these symbols to something this side of the eternal state, and their ingenuity has been taxed to the point of desperation in the pursuit of something that will answer the purpose. How well or how poorly they have succeeded we shall see as we advance.

In the Scriptures already considered we have found the same punishment indicated by the following terms and phrases: "*Gehenna*," "*Gehenna-fire*," "everlasting fire," "the fire that shall never be quenched;" and to these is added the significant allusion to the valley of Hinnom, the emblem of all that is horrible, "where their worm dieth not, and the fire is not quenched." Then, passing over to the period when the Son of man shall sit on the throne of his glory, and all nations shall be gathered before him, and he shall divide them as a shepherd divideth the sheep from the goats, and pronounce the final sentence against the wicked, we have that sentence in these words: "Depart from me, ye cursed, into everlasting fire, prepared for the devil and his angels." (Matt. xxv, 41.) Now, we think there can be no doubt that this "everlasting fire, prepared for the devil and his angels," is the same, and means the same thing, as the "everlasting fire" and the "*Gehenna-fire*" in the passages above. Of course, questions are raised on this passage about the coming of Christ, the nature of the gathering of the nations, the character of the judgment described, and all that; but, passing all these, we now hold our thought on the single point that the "everlasting fire, prepared for the devil and his angels," mean what it may, is the *Gehenna-fire* of the other Scriptures. This being settled, as settled it is in all unbiased minds, then the next point is, that this "fire, prepared for the devil and his angels," is the same in meaning as "the lake of fire" in the book of Revelation. That this is true, is evident from the following: "And the devil that deceived them was cast into the lake of fire and brimstone, where the beast and the false prophet are, and shall be tormented day and night forever and ever." (Rev. xx, 10.)

We are not now studying the nature or significance of these symbols nor their locality, but simply their relation to each other, and the identity of their import. It is a question of fact, to be determined by the nature of the case, by the similarity of expression and use, and by the unreasonableness of the supposition that such striking symbols, so nearly alike and relating to the same classes, and having the same uses, should not have the same final application and meaning. The devil is "cast into the lake of fire"—can there, then, be any doubt that this is the fire, "the everlasting fire," prepared for him? The beast and the false prophet are there, and all that may be designated as "his angels" will have their part in that lake; then how can it be otherwise than that this is the "everlasting fire prepared for the devil and his angels?" It seems preposterous, and even impossible, to doubt the fact here insisted upon. And yet if it be true, it brings the subject of *Gehenna* into such a light that its relation to the period beyond death, and beyond both the resurrection and the judgment, can no more be questioned. *Gehenna*, as we have seen, is not *Hades*, is not in *Hades*, is no part of *Hades*, and comes into the scenes of human destiny only as *Hades* goes out. Death and *Hades* deliver up their dead before the judgment, and after the judgment they are cast into the "lake of fire," which is *Gehenna*.

This point will bear repeating. In it centers the whole interest of this argument. Upon this single fact hinges much of the great debate concerning human destiny. To be cast into "the lake of fire" is the last calamity. It is "the second death." And is not the second death subsequent to the resurrection, and therefore in the future state? The following Scripture will determine: "And the sea gave up the dead which were in it; and *death* and *Hades* delivered up the dead which were in them; and they were judged every man according to their works. And *death* and *Hades* were cast into the lake of fire. This is the second death. And whosoever was not found written in the book of life was cast into the lake of fire." (Rev. xx, 13-15.) This passage has been considered before, and the order of events noted, but we must look again. 1. The great white throne appears, the emblem of judgment. 2. Heaven and earth flee away; the visible creation passes out of sight. 3. The dead, small and great, arise. All the receptacles of the dead, whether of body or soul, whether earth and sea, or *Hades*, the invisible world of spirits, deliver up their dead. 4. The judgment proceeds; the books—the records of Divine Providence and human life—are opened, and every man's real character is declared. 5. The ungodly are condemned—formally, judicially, as they have been morally—and sentenced, "Depart from me, ye cursed, into everlasting fire, prepared for the devil and his angels." 6. The sentence is executed. Death and *Hades*, and "whosoever was not found written in the book of life," were "cast into the lake of fire." "This is the second death." If the delivering up of the dead, here mentioned, is the resurrection of the dead, there is no escape from the conclusion that *Gehenna*, the lake of fire, and the second death, are all beyond the resurrection. But if the delivering up of the dead does not mean the resurrection, no one has ever yet succeeded in telling what it does mean, and nothing is hazarded in the prediction that no one ever will.

In the next chapter to this we find the "lake of fire" recognized in the immortal state, or in immediate connection with the new creation, when mortality and death are past. As this twentieth chapter closes up the history of this world, and notes the passing away of the visible creation, with "the righteous saved, the wicked damned, and

God's eternal government approved;" so the twenty-first chapter opens a new scene, where "the former things are done away"—a scene that lies beyond the limits of time: "And I saw a new heaven and a new earth; for the first heaven and the first earth were passed away; and there was no more sea. And I John saw the holy city, new Jerusalem, coming down from God out of heaven, prepared as a bride adorned for her husband. And I heard a great voice out of heaven, saying, Behold the tabernacle of God is with men, and he will dwell with them, and they shall be his people, and God himself shall be with them, and be their God. And God shall wipe away all tears from their eyes; and there shall be no more death, neither sorrow nor crying, neither shall there be any more pain; for the former things are passed away. And he that sat upon the throne said, Behold, I make all things new. And he said unto me, Write; for these words are true and faithful. And he said unto me, It is done. I am Alpha and Omega, the beginning and the end. I will give unto him that is athirst of the fountain of the water of life freely.

He that overcometh shall inherit all things; and I will be his God, and he shall be my son. But the fearful, and unbelieving, and the abominable, and murderers, and whoremongers, and sorcerers, and idolaters, and all liars, shall have their part in the lake which burneth with fire and brimstone; which is the second death." (Rev. xxi, 1–8.)

This new heaven and new earth are the inheritance of the saints after the resurrection of the dead. It is not all of heaven, nor all the heaven the saints shall know and enjoy; but it is their immortal home, where there is no death, nor sorrow, nor crying, nor pain; where God shall wipe away all tears, and dwell in the midst of his people. There is the city of the living God, the metropolis of the world of light, the home of all the saved. It can not be in time. It is not on earth beneath the curse of sin. It is not this world, but it is the world to come. And it is in connection with this new creation, in point of time, if the word time may be used in such connection, that the ungodly, the unsaved, "have their part in the lake that burneth with fire and brimstone; which is the second death." As certainly as this blessed state where there is no more curse nor death, where God wipes away all tears from the eyes of his people, is in the future world, so certainly is the state symbolized by the lake of fire in the future world. There is no "second death" till after the resurrection.

Now we have found *Gehenna*. If it is not yet created, it is ordained of old in the purpose of God, and when death delivers up the bodies, and *Hades* delivers up the souls of the unsaved, then after death, and after the resurrection, and after the judgment, "both soul and body" shall be "cast into *Gehenna*"— that real *Gehenna* of fire, the everlasting fire, prepared for the devil and his angels. The *name* means little to us; the thing is important, and had been just as real and as terrible if nameless. To the Jew the name was significant. It carried weight. To us the other symbol, the "lake of fire," is more impressive. The application is the same. The final destiny of the unsaved is the unsearchable reality.

The only escape for Universalism is to show that *Gehenna*, the "lake of fire," and the "second death," all relate to something this side of the resurrection of the dead. This is a vast undertaking, with immortal issues depending upon it, and has often been attempted, but never accomplished.

The first motion is to make the literal valley of Hinnom answer to all these forms of expression. But this is too preposterous to be depended on alone. It requires that we accept the assumption that the valley of Hinnom was the "fire prepared for the devil and his angels." And, further, it necessitates the belief that the "beast," and the "false prophet," and the devil were all cast into that valley, literally or figuratively, and that all the ungodly are condemned to the same fate. But who can believe this? It will also follow that the valley of Hinnom was the lake into which *death* and *Hades* were cast, after delivering up their dead. And who can believe that?

The next motion is to tell us that all these are figurative representations of the temporal judgments with which God visits the wicked, and especially of the destruction of Jerusalem. Well, then, what resemblance is there between the valley of Hinnom and the destruction of Jerusalem? Why did Christ tell the Jews, who believed in personal devils, that their national judgments were "prepared for the devil and his angels?" What temporal calamity was symbolized by the casting of the devil into the lake of fire, to be tormented day and night forever and ever? In what way could this represent the destruction of Jerusalem or any other temporal judgment? What temporal calamity is symbolized by the casting of *death* and *Hades* into the lake of fire? And if the casting of *death* and *Hades* into the lake of fire is a figurative setting forth of the abolishment of death and of the separate state of souls, as it undoubtedly is, how can this transaction be supposed to have taken place at the destruction of Jerusalem? Or how could it be used as a symbol of that calamitous event? Or why should the greater and more spiritual occurrence be taken as a figure of the smaller and more material one? Or, again, if this description of the destruction of *death* and *Hades*, be taken as relating to the destruction of Jerusalem, or to any other temporal calamity, what becomes of the argument for the universal restoration of humanity, founded on the destruction of *death* and *Hades*, in the resurrection? And if there is to be a destruction of *death* and *Hades* by the resurrection of the dead—as there certainly must be, if the dead rise at all—why should this language be applied to any thing else? And if the "lake of fire," be it what it may, appears and continues after the delivering up of the dead—as it surely does—how can it be on this side of the resurrection, or in any possible way relate to any thing on earth? If it is the receptacle of *death* and *Hades*, its place in the history of the universe is beyond the dominion of death, and beyond the period of the existence of souls in the disembodied state.

It is a light thing with "liberalists" to dispose of all these stern Scriptures by pronouncing them "figurative," and giving reasons why they must be taken in a figurative sense. We go with them in this, much farther than they allow their people to know or believe; for they wish it understood that "orthodox" people hold to the literal sense of this language, so that their superior light will the more readily impress their hearers; but, while we recognize symbols, metaphors, personifications, and other figures, wherever they exist, we seek to interpret and apply each passage according to its actual meaning, not omiting the figures. It is not satisfactory to show that a passage is figurative. We want to know what the figure means and what the passage means; and we want the figurative language to be so construed as to yield a sense in harmony with plainer passages, if possible, and never out of harmony with the tenor of Scripture teaching or doctrine.

But we are not through with the "liberalist" interpretations yet. We are sometimes told that the "lake of fire," and these other symbols, represent neither the destruction of Jerusalem nor other temporal judgments of a national or personal kind, but simply the *moral sufferings* to which sinners are liable. Well, can any one tell us what propriety there is in calling the moral sufferings of sinners in this world "the fire prepared for the devil and his angels?" Can any resemblance be found between the casting of the devil into the "lake of fire" and the moral sufferings of sinners in this world? May we not also ask what kind of moral sufferings were signified by the casting of *death* and *Hades* into the lake of fire? And if *Gehenna* is an emblem of moral sufferings, will not some one show us the point of resemblance which is the basis of the figure? And may we not further ask why the casting of the sinner into this state of moral suffering takes place only after the body is killed? and then why the body, as well as the soul, is included? And if the lake of fire is a symbol of moral sufferings, why is it placed beyond the destruction of *death* and *Hades*, and therefore beyond the resurrection of the dead, unless the moral sufferings are there also? But if the moral sufferings, symbolized by the "lake of fire," are indeed beyond the resurrection of the dead, and beyond the destruction of *death* and *Hades*, then is *Gehenna* there also; for *Gehenna* and "the lake of fire" point to the same sufferings. Let it be conceded that *Gehenna* and "the lake of fire" symbolize moral suffering beyond the destruction of *death* and *Hades*, and we ask no more. There is no resurrection beyond the resurrection. There is no destruction of death beyond the resurrection. There is no salvation from sin or death or suffering beyond the resurrection. If *Gehenna* is there, there also is "the everlasting fire," "the fire that shall never be quenched." Suppose the suffering is moral, Is it any the less real? Is it any the less terrible? Is it any the less final? Is not subjective wretchedness penal?

Finally, on this point, we are told by "liberalists," that the "lake of fire" denotes a process of purification, and that all the abominable characters of earth who have "their part" therein enjoy a great benefit! This lake is styled "a sovereign fire for purification," and the declaration that ungodly men shall have part therein, is construed into a most precious promise and pledge of what God shall do for all those who reject Christ! Then shall we any longer ridicule the Romish dogma of Purgatory? Does not this exceed the absurdity of that doctrine by far? Romanists find their Purgatory this side of the burning lake, while *Hades* yet exists before death is destroyed, and before the final judgment is past. But, with less reason, and less regard to Scriptural warrant, and without consistency of interpretation, "liberalists" find a purgatory in the perdition of ungodly men. We confess to astonishment at such temerity, and stand appalled before such wresting of the Scriptures.

If the "lake of fire" denotes a process of purification, so does *Gehenna*, for this can not in reason be used differently, much less in an opposite sense. And the same is true of the "second death," for that consists in being cast into the lake. Then also must we ask, How comes it that this process of purification, set forth under emblems of the severest punishment, reached in consequence of rejecting the Gospel remedies for sin, is reserved until after the resurrection of the dead, and after the destruction of *death* and *Hades?* Although, in fact, there is no ground in Scripture on which to affirm a fiery ordeal of purification in *Hades*, it is far more reasonable to conjecture that such a process is possible there than in *Gehenna*. If any form of probation continues after death, it is unquestionably found in the unseen world, and on this side of the destruction of *Hades;* so that the admission of another trial does not antagonize the doctrine of the finality of the punishment in *Gehenna,* of which the lake of fire is so impressive an emblem. If any are put on probation again, it must be those who have not had the Gospel in this life,—not those who have rejected it,—and if probation fails here, it may there. If the Gospel is rejected, and the divine Redeemer set at naught, the penal fires of the invisible world may also be defied, and all the reformatory agencies of *Hades* may prove inadequate to secure the regeneration of men, whose aggravated obstinacy, gathered in the idolatries and sensualities of earth, has gone with them into the state of the dead. With such the transition from *Hades* to *Gehenna* will not indicate improvement. Their moral affinities must be for evil, and their tendencies downward. By the operation of moral gravitation they sink forever.

The assumption is that the "lake of fire" is a "process of purification." Then all that are cast into it are sent there for the purpose of purification. The "beast and the false prophet" are there. When will they be purified? The devil is to be cast into it. Will he be purified? Why not? Death and *Hades* are to be cast into it. Is this for the purpose of purification? "But these are to be destroyed," I hear it said. Then, why cast them into "a sovereign fire for purification?" Consistency should be observed in the use of figures of speech and in the disposition of symbols. But if we admit the destruction of these, what then? The beast and false prophet were cast into the lake of fire and destroyed. The devil was cast into the lake of fire and destroyed. Death and *Hades* were cast into the lake of fire and destroyed— abolished forever. "Whosoever was not found written in the book of life was cast into the lake of fire," and—and purified!

Perhaps some will deny the material point in this connection; that is, that *Gehenna* and the lake of fire mean the same thing. If they do, the difficulties are not canceled. The formidable facts of Scripture confront them still. The "lake of fire" is there, the emblem of the final state of the wicked, beyond the resurrection and the judgment; and whatever meaning is attached to *Gehenna*, and however figurative the "lake of fire," the point so clearly made, that the punishment denoted is in the future world, stands unmoved. And this is the great fact. Then, what if it could be shown that by the use of *Gehenna* the Savior made the valley of Hinnom the emblem of national judgments? Would that explain the doom of the devil, and all the punishments that follow the destruction of *death* and *Hades?* Would it obliterate the significance of the "second death?"

But no good reason can be given for separating *Gehenna* and the lake of fire. As we have seen, *Gehenna* means punishment after death. Men are cast into it after the body is killed; and yet it receives them, soul and body, together. It is therefore after the resurrection. It is the *Gehenna-fire*—"the everlasting fire," "the unquenchable fire," and it is the "fire prepared for the devil and his angels." It corresponds in every particular to the "lake of fire." Like the lake, it is after death, after the resurrection, and after the judgment; and it receives the devil and his angels, as well as the ungodly of earth. Then why separate them? This can not be done. *Gehenna* and the "lake of fire" point to the same thing. That thing is final. It is the "second death." Upon it falls the curtain of everlasting night! No voice echoes back its horrors. No light gleams from its lurid burnings. No revolution of cycles numbers the measure of its years. Eternity, dark, fathomless, hopeless, seals the fate of all adjudged to dwell amid the devouring fires.

Chapter XV.

THE SECOND DEATH.

IT is almost superfluous to add a chapter under the above caption, and yet there are two or three points that ought to be considered.

The "second death," as was shown in the preceding chapter, relates to the "lake of fire," and expresses the last calamity of the wicked. The point in question concerning it has reference to the time when it shall occur, and the relation in which it stands to other events which mark the winding up of the Gospel economy, and the ushering in of the unchangeable realities of eternity. If we have read the Scriptures correctly, it is to occur beyond the mediatorial reign of Christ, beyond the end of time, beyond the period of the separate existence of the soul in *Hades*, beyond the resurrection of the dead, and beyond the final judgment. All this has been made to appear, so that all that now remains is to consider what objectors,—and especially Universalists,—have had to say in regard to it.

Writers of the "liberalistic" class have usually skipped over this phraseology as lightly as possible. But few have positively expressed themselves in relation to it. Rev. J. M. Austin, in discussion with Dr. Holmes, says: "The second death is a figurative form of speech, used by the Revelator, unquestionably, with reference to God's dealings with the Jews. It was a national death. The first death of that people was their Babylonian captivity." This is significant. It shows timidity. It does not affirm any thing, but leaves us to infer that the "second death" means the national overthrow of the Jews by the Romans. This opinion, or rather suggestion, is shared by very many. It seems to answer a purpose. It puts a meaning on the phrase. But is it sound? Is it consistent? Does it explain the Scriptural use of the phrase? How is it supported?

If the "second death" is a national event,

so also is the "lake of fire." But in the national captivity, which this man tells us was the "first death" of the Jews, the good and bad were alike involved; and so it is very largely in all national calamities. Are we to believe that the good and bad share alike in the "second death?" Are they alike cast into the lake of fire? Did the beast and false prophet represent the Jewish nationality? Was the devil a partaker in the national downfall of the Jews? These are all cast into the lake of fire, and this is the "second death." But if the second death is a national death of the Jews, accomplished when Jerusalem was destroyed, why is it, in the symbolical representation, put off till after the termination of the existence in *Hades?* Why is it placed beyond the destruction of death? Why do we find it only beyond the resurrection and the judgment? This order of events is not accidental. It is too uniform and too clearly put in the account to be treated as destitute of meaning. To it we appeal with confidence. It forever sets aside all arbitrary applications of the "second death" to any national event in the history of the past.

Others of the same school teach differently. Rev. I. D. Williamson, D. D., widely known as author and editor in the Universalist ranks, and of excellent reputation, thus presents the subject: "There were some in the days of Jude who suffered this death. Speaking of those unbelieving Jews who turned the grace of God into lasciviousness, and denied the Lord that bought them, he says, 'These are spots in your feasts of charity; clouds without water, driven about with winds; trees whose fruit withereth, twice dead, plucked up by the roots.' *Twice* dead, did the apostle say? Aye, verily. Then they had suffered the 'second death.' The Gospel found them dead in sin. By its quickening energies it raised them to spiritual life. But now they rejected the Gospel, denied the Lord that bought them, and were hurt of the second death. Such are my views of the second death, and of their correctness I entertain no manner of doubt." (Lectures, page 161.)

The point here is readily seen, and its want of force is easily shown. It makes the second death consist in backsliding or apostasy; and the only foundation it has is in the metaphorical tree which is spoken of as "twice dead." But there is no proof that the persons represented by the fruitless trees were ever converted or raised by the quickening energies of the Gospel to spiritual life. The indications in the passage and in the connection are all against the supposition. These persons are described in the fourth verse, part of which the doctor applies to them, and so well identified that we dare not admit that they ever were truly converted. They appear to have gotten into the Church, or in some way to have sought association with the disciples, but not by right as sincere inquirers or genuine converts. "For there are certain men crept in unawares, who were before of old ordained to this condemnation, ungodly men, turning the grace of our God into lasciviousness, and denying the only Lord God, and our Lord Jesus Christ." They were not converts, but "ungodly men;" they "crept in unawares." There is not a solitary hint in all the book that they were converted. Then, of course, they were not backsliders. Every thing in the account marks them as impostors. So bad were they that the apostle seems to have labored to find metaphors strong enough to picture their utter worthlessness; and in quoting the passage our author omits some of the terrible arraignment. Let us read it entire: "These are spots in your feasts of charity, when they feast with you, feeding themselves without fear; clouds they are without water, carried about of winds; trees whose fruit withereth, without fruit, twice dead, plucked up by the roots; raging waves of the sea, foaming out their own shame; wandering stars, to whom is reserved the blackness of darkness forever." They are "spots;" they are "clouds;" they are "trees;" they are "raging waves of the sea;" they are "wandering stars." As "clouds" they are "without water;" and as "trees" they are "without fruit, twice dead, plucked up by the roots." The "twice dead" is simply an emphatic representation of their utter destitution of life, and this is intensified further by the next expression, "plucked up by the roots." Thus the apostle shows their absolute hopelessness, so far as fruit-bearing is concerned. If any thing in the passage is plain, it is that these "ungodly men," who "crept in unawares," were never in the Church by right, but were deceivers from the beginning. They are fully described, and not less graphically or forcibly, in the second chapter of the second epistle of Peter.

But even if the apostle was speaking of backsliders, the phrase "twice dead," descriptive of the fruitless trees, as it is, is an insufficient warrant for this interpretation of the second death. There is no hint in all the Bible that the "second death" is restricted to backsliders. On the contrary, it is affirmed of all who "were not found written in the book of life;" in Revelation xxi, 8, we have at least a partial catalogue of the characters destined to the dreadful experience. This includes many who were never converted. The hypothesis is contradicted by every passage that mentions the subject. And besides all this, the period of the "second death," as determined by the order of events, is beyond the limits of this life; for it is never recognized in the New Testament except as following the resurrection of the dead. It consists in being cast into the lake of fire. That lake, symbol though it be, does not appear till after the separate existence in *Hades*, and after the reign of death over the bodies of men. It is the last calamity. Nothing is revealed beyond it.

Its nature and results are not in our present inquiry. Evidently it cuts off all hope of eternal life. Some think it destroys the body, and separates the soul from it, leaving the latter to its wandering loneliness in the darkness of space, beyond the boundaries of the organic universe—"the blackness of darkness forever" being its sole inheritance. This, however, is speculation. Our present business is with facts. The second death is a fact of stupendous import. Its incidents are unknown, and may we never come into the awful secret of its power and effect! One thing we know, and that is, it is not the way to heaven. There is no intimation in all the Scriptures that any human soul ever did or ever can pass its portals and enter the gates of the city of God. The song of triumph before the throne recalls the redemption from earth, and sin, and death, but not from the "second death."

Chapter XVI.

RESURRECTION OF DAMNATION.

THIS is Scriptural language, and it means something. It will, therefore, be profitable for us to study it, and, if possible, find out its real import. The passage is as follows: "Marvel not at this; for the hour is coming in which all that are in the graves shall hear his voice, and shall come forth; they that have done good unto the resurrection of life, and they that have done evil, unto the resurrection of damnation."

Almost every one who has a doctrine to maintain, whether orthodox or heterodox, finds it necessary to explain these words, either to apply them to the support of his position, or to get them out of his way; and, unfortunately, the most that has been written on the passage, has had the latter object in view. Universalists have had great trouble with this

Scripture, and their abuse of it is wonderful. Swedenborgians, Quakers, Second Adventists, and all the hosts of Destructionists and Liberalists, who deny the resurrection of the bodies of the wicked, find it a lion in their path, looking them steadily in the face, and defying their skill. Professor Bush, who has distinguished himself perhaps more than any other man in a century, in opposing the doctrine of the resurrection of the body, found great difficulty in attempting to harmonize these words with his predetermined conclusions. He says: "The passage, as understood in its literal import, does certainly encounter the force of that cumulative mass of evidence, built upon rational and philosophical grounds, which we have arrayed against any statement of the doctrine that would imply the participation of the body in the rising again which is predicated of the dead. We do not, by any means, affirm that the conclusions from that source to which we have come are sufficient of themselves to countervail the rebutting conclusions which may be formed from the present text. All we would say is, that they have weight, and, consequently, we are not required, or rather are not at liberty, at once to dismiss them." Strange that he did not see that a plain "thus saith the Lord" should sweep away all "conclusions" the moment it encountered them, which were based on merely "rational and philosophical grounds;" but when men set out to oppose their rational deductions to God's miracles, there is no limit to their fallacies or to their infatuations.

We shall not examine all that has been said by various parties in order to break the force of this Scripture in support of the literal resurrection of the dead; for, while they approach it with different ends to serve, or it may be with conflicting conclusions to support, they agree in trying to explain it without taking it in its most obvious sense, as proclaiming a general rising again of the good and bad. Therefore a consideration of the common methods of interpretation will suffice, without specific reference to the doctrines of the different opposers of the literal sense.

All who object to the literal sense for some reason deny the literal resurrection, and mostly because this "coming forth unto a resurrection of damnation" carries along with it the idea of eternal punishment, or of the irrevocable condemnation of the wicked, in the eternal world. Denying this doctrine, they are compelled to fix upon the passage some kind of interpretation which assumes that the language is figurative; and we find them not at all particular about the figure, so it is "figurative," and does not mean what it says. Their most common method is to appeal to the Old Testament writers, particularly Daniel and Ezekiel, to explain these words of the New Testament. They would have these old prophets explain Christ!

We protest against this, as a reversal of the order of things. It violates one of the most important rules of exegesis, in making the older and more obscure writers limit and explain the meaning of the later and plainer ones. This is manifestly improper. Not, indeed, that the Old Testament can not shed light upon the New, where there is a connection between them, or an allusion in the New to the Old; in many instances it does: but the language of the Old is not to be made the standard by which the language of the New is to be tried. The later and plainer sayings of Christ, and of the New Testament writers, should be taken as the commentary, and not the reverse of this, if there be in them any allusion to the prophecies of the Old Testament. Our Savior should be allowed to explain Daniel and Ezekiel, even to the extent, if need be, of giving their words an application beyond any thing they knew or intended; for he came after them, and understood them, and had the right to enlarge their meaning, which he often did, not by contradicting their utterances, but by expanding them and lifting them to a higher plane of thought, where spiritual and eternal truths come into view, in addition to the temporalities which filled the vision of the prophets. We dare not therefore restrict the words of Christ to the precise scope and meaning of similar language in the Old Testament.

If the words of Christ before us, allude at all to the passage in Daniel, they are an authoritative exposition and application of that passage; and if they allude to the vision of "dry bones" in Ezekiel, they must be taken as an explanation of the ultimate meaning of that prophecy. With this remark, the correctness and fairness of which is beyond question, we may look at these Old Testament Scriptures and see how impossible it is, even with their assistance, to escape the doctrine of a general resurrection followed by eternal retributions.

"And at that time shall Michael stand up, the great prince which standeth for the children of thy people; and there shall be a time of trouble, such as never was since there was a nation, even to that same time: and at that time thy people shall be delivered, every one that shall be found written in the book. And many of them that sleep in the dust of the earth shall awake; some to everlasting life, and some to shame and everlasting contempt." (Dan. xii, 1, 2.) The phrase, "many of them that sleep," is equivalent to "the many," or "as many of them that sleep;" so that the language does not forbid the idea of a general rising, but rather implies it. There is no doubt that it relates to a resurrection of some kind, and to some extent, and one in which there are two classes sharing, and two opposite results following. What does it mean?

The objectors to the literal resurrection assume, of course, that it means a "figurative" resurrection, or that the language is "figurative," and means something which is a resurrection only in a figurative sense. Well, what does it all mean? Some tell us that it means a political resurrection, and others insist that it relates to a moral or spiritual resurrection. We shall test both interpretations.

But finding what we wish to say on this point well said by Dr. Kingsley—subsequently bishop—we quote his words: "But is the passage which we have quoted from Daniel figurative? If so, what does the sleep or death in the dust mean? Whatever it means, to awake and come out of the dust must mean the very reverse. Well, then, suppose it means *political* death—political degradation and adversity. Then to come forth from this death would be to enjoy a life of political prosperity. But some 'awake to shame and everlasting contempt.' What kind of political prosperity is this? Political shame and contempt are just what the political death signifies. Are the death and the resurrection from death the same thing? Then it can not mean a political death. Let us see whether *spiritual* death will do any better. If the death is a death in trespasses and sins, then awaking from this death is coming forth to a life of purity and holiness. But some that were dead 'awake to shame and everlasting contempt.' What kind of purity and holiness is this? How hard it is to make God's Word teach false doctrines!"

All this and more comes from the attempt to explain the words of Christ, which are so plain and pointed, by the less plain and more highly figurative language of the old prophet. Now, let us reverse this order, and permit the Savior, the later speaker, to explain the words of the former speaker. It then appears that the "many that sleep in the dust of the earth," means "all that are in the graves;" that they "awake" by hearing the "voice of the Son of God;" that to "awake to everlasting life" means to "come forth unto the resurrection of life," and that to "awake to shame and everlasting contempt" is to "come forth unto the resurrection of damnation." This is plain, consistent, natural, and if left untortured, its meaning is easily understood.

But our "liberalistic" friends not only labor to limit this passage by the language quoted from Daniel, explaining the plain by the obscure, but they seek with much exertion to interpret it by Ezekiel's vision of "dry bones"—claiming, of course, that it means neither more nor less than that vision signifies. This is all gratuitous. There is no allusion in the passage in John to that vision in Ezekiel; but if such allusion could be found, the words of Christ would have to be taken as an authoritative exposition of that vision, giving to it an ultimate meaning quite beyond its primary design, and possibly reaching beyond the prophet's highest conception of its import.

Ezekiel's language is necessarily figurative. It carries evidence of this upon its face, as it can not possibly be explained except as figurative language. But this is not the case with the language of Christ, as there is nothing in it inconsistent with a literal interpretation. Ezekiel spoke of the "whole house of Israel;" but Christ spoke of "all that are in the graves." Ezekiel spoke of the rising of only one class, while Christ spoke definitely of the resurrection of two classes, the good and the bad. Ezekiel prophesied long before the birth of Christ, and neither he nor the other prophets brought "life and immortality to light" so clearly as did the Messiah himself. The latter came after the prophets, and was in every respect greater than the prophets, and made many things plain which the prophets left obscure. He fulfilled many of their predictions, and poured light upon what they only darkly shadowed forth; confirming their words, indeed, but giving them an application and meaning truly his own. Then, how absurd the attempt to make his words subordinate to theirs—or, which is the same thing, to restrict the import of his language by the necessary limitations of theirs!

The words of Christ, in this passage in John, mean more than did Ezekiel's vision of "dry bones," or they do not. If they do not, they relate to the moral reformation of Israel before Christ was born, and to the consequent restoration of the nation from the "Babylonian captivity," which was accomplished hundreds of years before the words were spoken by him, although he clearly intimated that he was looking to the future, saying, "the hour is coming." But if his words do mean more than that vision meant, then it is manifest folly to try to explain them by that vision, or to restrict them to its signification. Ezekiel's vision represented the house of Israel in their backslidden condition, as in a state of spiritual death and their captivity as a political death. They had apostatized, and they had been carried away to Babylon; and now they were repenting, and God was about to deliver them from bondage, and restore them to their land and their nationality. The prophet, in this vision, described their repentance and return, under the figure of a resurrection from the dead. It was a deliverance from the moral and political death they had suffered. The moral resurrection is indicated in these words: "And I shall put my spirit in you, and ye shall live." The political resurrection is expressed thus: "I will open your graves, and cause you to come up out of your graves into the land of Israel, and I shall place you in your own land." But in all this there is not a word about the "resurrection of damnation." This much, at least, the Savior added, and this is the point of difficulty with all who seek a figurative interpretation for his words. They could make the word "damnation" represent a state of apostasy, or any adverse or degraded condition, politically or morally considered; but how to manage the word "resurrection," in this connection, is what they are unable to find.

Then, having seen the absurdity of limiting this passage in John to the exact import of similar language in the Old Testament, we come to a direct examination of the efforts which have been made to give it other than its plain, literal meaning.

It is sometimes claimed that it should be understood of a spiritual resurrection, because a spiritual resurrection is taught in this chapter, and was largely the subject of discourse on this particular occasion. But this fact, when examined, furnishes a substantial reason why the claim should not be admitted. The Savior was not guilty of "vain repetitions," and did not indulge in useless tautology. Hence, having taught the doctrine of a spiritual death and resurrection, as plainly appears in the twenty-fourth and twenty-fifth verses of this chapter, he certainly did not proceed, in these next verses, to declare the same thing over again in language less easily understood. We could not believe him guilty of such a departure from the propriety of speech, even if we had no warning against it. But we have warning against it. The phrase, "marvel not at this," forbids the idea that he was just going to repeat the same thing in different language, and requires us to suppose he had finished the point in hand, and was about to tell them something different and still more wonderful. He had just said to them, "The time is now come when the spiritually dead shall hear the voice of the Son of God, and they that truly hear shall be made alive to God by faith," and this marvelous announcement no doubt caused signs of astonishment to appear in his audience, which he recognized, and to which he alluded, when he proceeded not to tell the same thing, but to make the still more astounding revelation. He continued, "Marvel not at this," it is a great mystery, but not so startling as that which is yet to come—"Marvel not at this; for the hour is coming in the which all that are in the graves shall hear his voice, and shall come forth." This is truly marvelous! Nothing but infinite power and wisdom can accomplish it; nevertheless it is positively affirmed, and it is carefully distinguished from the spiritual resurrection. In the twenty-fourth and twenty-fifth verses, the language relates to a present privilege, as is seen in a note of time which should not be overlooked. "Verily, verily I say unto you, the hour is coming, *and now is*." There can be no mistake here. But in the passage which describes the more marvelous event, there is no such indication of time. It is simply, "The hour is coming." The omission of the phrase "and now is," is significant. It places the "coming forth" from the "graves" in the future, and not in the present.

Those who are spiritually dead, or "dead in trespasses and in sins," are not in condition to do good, nor does the Bible ascribe good works to them while in that state. They first "pass from death unto life."

They must hear the voice of the Son of God, as he speaks to them through the Gospel, receive his quickening grace, and then begin a course of good works as the fruit of faith. But some of those mentioned in the twenty-eighth verse had "done good," not while in the grave, of course, but before going into it, and before hearing the voice of the Son of God calling them to come forth. Their having "done good" is that which now distinguishes them, and secures the divine approval; not that it secures the "coming forth," but it determines the character and results of the resurrection, giving them part in the "resurrection of life." They that have "done evil" shall also hear the voice and come forth, but unto a very different resurrection. Then, if we suppose this whole passage speaks of a spiritual death and resurrection, what are we to understand by this "coming forth unto a resurrection of damnation?" We are told that the last word means "condemnation." Very well; but were not those who had "done evil" condemned before this coming forth? We read that unbelievers are "condemned already."

But this is not the word whose meaning we are seeking after, for no stress is laid on any difference, supposed or real, between damnation and condemnation. The question is, What idea shall we attach to the word "resurrection" in this remarkable sentence? There is evidently a resurrection in contemplation for those already condemned, for they "shall come forth;" now, what does this mean? If they are spiritually dead, and in the graves of sin, no coming forth is needed to bring them into condemnation; nor can we conceive of any coming forth from the graves of sin without a deliverance from sin, and therefore from condemnation. This would be to emerge into a life of holiness; but no such coming forth into life is predicated of them.

At this point "liberalists" resort to quibbling. They tell us that all of us do some good and some evil during life, so that if this passage be taken literally, we must all have part in both resurrections. This is a play upon words. To all sensible people it is clear enough that there are two classes here, distinguished by their predominant characteristics, as the good and bad; and that these include all the race, indicating their relation to Christ, without marking the quality or measure of their moral deserts, further than to denote the fact of their classification. Hence, "they that have done good" will not include such as once did a good thing or a number of good things and then rejected Christ, and died impenitent. In that event the Scriptures inform us that their former righteousness shall not be remembered unto them. And "they that have done evil" will not include those who for a time lived in sin, and afterwards repented and obtained pardon; for their sins are "blotted out," and shall be remembered no more forever. Those who put this forward as a difficulty overlook the fact that if there be any trouble in it in the interpretation of the passage of a literal resurrection, the same trouble exists in the way of the spiritual resurrection.

Another point of about the same character, and usually mentioned in the same connection, is the assertion that these words can not refer to all the dead, and teach a general resurrection, for the reason that some are not "in the graves," having never been buried.

Some are lost in the sea, some are burned to ashes, and some are left to putrefaction above ground; but then the word "graves" denotes the resting-place of human dust, wherever it may lie in the broad empire of death. The sea, death, and *Hades* shall deliver up the dead which are in them. Then, again, we are told that this Scripture does not relate to a resurrection from either bodily or spiritual death, but to an elevation of the Church from poverty and reproach to a high position of honor and influence in the world. Learned disquisitions are given to prove that the word resurrection means promotion, or a going up to a higher state. With Universalists this is a favorite thought, especially when they encounter the passage which speaks of men being "recompensed in the resurrection of the just." At all hazards they must escape the idea of any "recompense" in the resurrection state, for either good or bad. But if the elevation of the Church in this world to a state of prosperity and happiness constitutes the "coming forth unto the resurrection of life," the question recurs with undiminished force, What does the "coming forth unto the resurrection of damnation" mean? What sort of "promotion" or elevation is this? In answer we hear it said, that in times of the Church's triumph the wicked hear the Gospel, reject it, and sink into deeper guilt and degradation. And so they do; but if the word resurrection means promotion or elevation, not to say rising from the dominion of death, we fail to see why it should be employed to express this experience of sinking deeper and deeper into moral darkness and misery. This is a strange promotion indeed!

But, finally, losing confidence in all other efforts to explain away this terrible "resurrection of damnation," Liberalists adopt the short method of disposing of it by applying the whole passage to national affairs. With them the destruction of Jerusalem solves all mysteries. The "resurrection of life" is made to mean the calling of the Gentiles to inherit Gospel privileges and blessings, while the "resurrection of damnation" is referred to the overthrow of the Jews, when their city and temple were destroyed by the Roman army. But, unfortunately for this notion, the

Gentiles had not "done good" prior to their call, nor was their call based on their former good conduct at all. This application, therefore, is both unwarranted and preposterous. So, in the downfall of the Jews, we can see "condemnation" easily enough, but we find nothing like a "coming forth" from the graves—nothing to designate as a "resurrection," even in the sense of "promotion." In a word, every effort to explain this passage of Scripture without accepting the literal meaning—that is, without applying it to the general resurrection of the dead, to be followed by eternal retributions, is a manifest failure. The clear, steady current of truth sweeps away all these devices of error, like drift upon the flowing stream, leaving no resort for the believer in the Scriptures, but to acknowledge the fact that the "hour is coming, in the which all that are in the graves shall hear his voice, and shall come forth; they that have done good unto the resurrection of life; and they that have done evil unto the resurrection of damnation." This is "the second death," the "*damnation of Gehenna.*"

www.ingramcontent.com/pod-product-compliance
Lightning Source LLC
Chambersburg PA
CBHW031935230426
43672CB00010B/1935